the rise

OF NATIONAL POPULISM AND DEMOCRATIC SOCIALISM

What Our Response
Should Be

the rise

OF NATIONAL POPULISM AND DEMOCRATIC SOCIALISM

What Our Response Should Be

Thomas Donelson

Post Hill Press
New York • Nashville
posthillpress.com

Published in the United States of America

Contents

Foreword

This book deals with the aftermath of the 2016 elections. It begins by describing the rise of Democratic Socialism and National Populism and the effect of these two ideas on our politics in 2016 and beyond. We reviewed data collected from our surveys on what voters believe, and conclude with asking what path we take from here.

Americas Majority Foundation, where I serve as a research associate and project director, surveyed 70,000 voters since the 2014 elections including after the 2016 elections. We found that many Americans rejected Obamanomics: Keynesian economics on steroids. They doubted if increasing government spending would either help the economy or their opportunity to succeed. They believed that America's role in the world did affect our economy at home and our ability to deter our enemies abroad. The one piece of survey data that predicted the rise of Donald Trump and Bernie Sanders was that three-quarters of voters viewed the system was rigged against the middle class.

Trump and Sanders based their entire campaign on this premise—screw those forces that screwed the middle class. Sanders's campaign based his premise that the "one percent" were stealing from the rest of us and his campaign featured an attack on the producers of America's wealth. Sanders forced the Democrats into becoming a Democratic Socialist party.

Trump brought nationalist populism into the Republican Party and while Trump has made reform of our federal government a priority, he is not a major proponent of shrinking government or entitlement reform. Trump, unlike Sanders, didn't have a 30-point plan and he never expressed a consistent ideology other than "make America great." (The exception is trade, where he viewed bad trade deals as hurting the middle class.)

Trump's nationalism does have similarity to Sanders's Democratic Socialism in that both agree the middle class have been hurt by trade deals and party elites and the new enemy are the globalists with their support for unlimited immigration and free trade. Trump's National Populism differs from Democratic Socialism because Trump actually likes America and he has no intention of surrendering American sovereignty to transnational organizations. After Obama allowed the UN to vote against Israel during the transition period, many Americans may be ready to rethink their commitments to international organizations like the UN and Trump may be ready to lead them out of these organizations just as he did leaving the Paris accord on climate change.

This book also discusses the conservative response to the rise of National Populism and Democratic Socialism. Trump's own agenda does have synergy with many conservative goals including education reform, increasing energy production, reducing taxes, and reforming government. While there are issues that conservatives and Trump will not agree, there is a consensus already reached on many key issues.

On foreign affairs, Trump offers an opportunity to revise American foreign policy, beginning with supporting Brexit. Britain leaving the European Union gives the United States an opportunity to advance a new alliance, the Anglosphere, in which the English-speaking nations form their own coalition.

The biggest threat of National Populism is that many within the movement are not prepared to shrink government but instead, use government to reward its supporters. The support for infrastructure expansion, for example, is based on Keynesian job creation theories that resulted in very little during the first Obama administration.

The "alt-right," a small group of white supremacists, has hooked onto the National Populist movement to enhance their influence. The alt-right movement is not conservative or an alternative to conservatism but nothing more than white supremacist fascists who hate the Constitution and free markets. They are closer to the Democratic Socialist movement than the conservative movement with their emphasis on White identity politics, similar to the Democratic Socialist movement's stress on racial identity politics. It is important for conservatives to distance themselves from the alt-right or we may be considered allies of racism. It is equally important to remember the alt-right is but a splinter and represent far less threat to our democracy than the various antifascist street gangs who has kept conservatives from speaking on college campus and other acts of violence.

The biggest threat to America is the Democratic Socialist movement, as the left's ever-expanding desire to grow government threaten our basic freedoms. The bureaucratic state has usurped the power of our elected officials and the left has used our government to attack their opponents through the IRS and other agencies.

The good news is that as our research shows, Americans have rejected the left's views. The Obama years produced a slow growing recovery that failed to lift the average American's income. Obama's failures in foreign policy have awakened many Americans to their vulnerability, as we are less secure today than when Obama took office and the world is more chaotic.

The left still feels emboldened and the next four years will be crucial for America. As the last eight years and the last election showed, the left will use whatever weapons they have to ensure the failure of the Trump Administration including impeachment on dubious charges. They have not truly accepted the election results and with excuses from Russian hacking to "fake news," their view is that this election is just a bump in the road toward a Democratic Socialist future.

As the Trump years begin, we have the issues on our side and that is a start. With the issues on our side, we can begin the process of stopping the left's march and work to transform this country into that land that once again stands as a beacon of hope. This book is dedicated to the premise that we can triumph but only if we understand the right lessons from the 2016 election.

CHAPTER ONE

The Rise of National Populism and Democratic Socialism

The appeal of National Populism and Democratic Socialism is both acknowledge the fears and anxieties of large swaths of the electorate and provide *fresh sounding* solutions to the problems voters are facing. But despite being *fresh sounding*, the solutions are actually old, have been tried and found wanting. But compared to the stale 40-year-old rhetoric of main-line Republican and Democratic politicians, National Populism and Democratic Socialism seem like new solutions to the voter's problems.

Democratic Socialism and National Populism grow from the same roots—a low-growth economy in the US, stagnant wages, and flat productivity because the Industrial Revolution is now mature. In addition, the U.S. has to compete against every other country in the world. The main difference between Democratic Socialism and National Populism is the narratives they tell and how they position their brands, how they reflect the anxieties and aspirations of their supporters, and whom they blame for life's challenges and disappointments. Humans need a narrative to understand the world, which means there must be a victim, a villain, and a hero. National Populism and Democratic Socialism have almost the same MacGuffin, but different characters to fill the roles of victim, villain, and hero.

National Populism appeals to people who hold traditional values— patriotism, the dignity of hard work, the respect of Christian faith, and the importance of the traditional family. The values that Illinois State University historian Andrew Hartman described as, "values that middle-class whites recognized as their own."[1] In the National Populist narrative, the victims are people who work hard and follow the traditional values of the middle class. The villains are "the Establishment" and various "losers" who have rigged or screwed up the system so much, following the rules no longer works. The heroes are Donald Trump and his supporters who are standing up to the establishment to Make America Great Again.

Trump voters come from every faction of the Republican Party: conservatives, moderates, and liberals. These voters wanted leaders who took their concerns seriously and did not mock their values. If translated into policy, National Populism benefits workers in industries the government favors for protection, businesses that cannot sustain foreign competition, companies holding government-backed debt, and companies willing to collude with the government for business advantages.

Democratic Socialism appeals to people who hold Progressive values—multiculturalism, social justice, equality of outcomes, a belief that smart technocrats can create a more just world, and a belief in "spirituality" in place of organized religion. In their narrative, the victims are nearly everyone but white men and the villains are white men, especially those who work at investment banks or are leaders of large, Old Economy companies who have rigged the system so they win and everyone else loses. Their heroes are campus protestors, liberal activists, and government technocrats.

In practice Democrat Socialism benefits government employees and their pension plans, green technology companies, people receiving direct government benefits, individuals with government guaranteed mortgages or student loans, workers in competitive global industries and companies whose businesses models can succeed through near monopoly status by making the concessions needed to come under the government umbrella.

There is significant overlap between Sanders's Democrat Socialism and Trump's National Populism. As Charles Murray opined in the *Wall Street Journal*, "*If Bernie Sanders were passionate about immigration, the rest of his ideology would have a lot more in common with Trumpism than conservatism does.*"[2]

The risks and dangers of National Populism and Democrat Socialism are not what Trump or Sanders would do if elected—the Conservative Republican House and Democrats in the Senate will ensure there is gridlock when it comes to statutes and appropriations. The threat is how Trump and Sanders supporters will react after several more years of their complaints not being acted upon. For conservatives, the fear should be the loss of 35 percent of Republican voters. A Trump takeover of the Republican Party would be a dream for liberals, creating a political landscape in which the conservatives and libertarians are moved to the sidelines as two leftist parties fight it out.

Together, Democrat Socialism and National Populism could form a winning coalition, or a governing legislative consensus and be the fatal blow to what remains of the American Creed.

National Populism

The core values of the American Creed, as articulated by American Enterprise Institute fellow Charles Murray, emphasize an opportunity state buttressed by liberty and individual rights, including equality before the law, freedom of speech and association, and economic opportunity through limited government and free market economics. There was a time when the creed was the consensus view of both major political parties. America had a belief in egalitarianism in which all were equal before the law and no one was better than anyone else.

Trumpism may threaten this Creed. Trumpism is flourishing at a time in which a new lower class is emerging within the white working class as work and marriage decline. White working-class men in their thirties and forties saw their labor participation drop from 96 percent to 79 percent since 1968 while marriage rate dropped from 86 percent to 52 percent in that same time period. One out of every five men in these prime working years are no longer looking for work and they have lost faith in the Republican Party. They view Trump as their final hope. To quote Charles Murray, "*There is nothing conservative about how they want to fix things. They want a now indifferent government to act on their behalf, big time.*"[3]

For many of these individuals, they blame free trade for a closed factory or illegal immigrants for loss of their jobs on local construction projects. Many Trump supporters are abandoning conservatism and they no longer believe in the American Creed—*but then many of the elites that look down upon them don't believe in the American Creed either.*

National Populism's appeal is that provides easy, clear-sounding, government-driven solutions to the deep economic headwinds of our time. In the National Populist narrative, all that is needed for jobs to come back are a few votes in Congress: tariffs to keep out foreign goods, incentives to bring back manufacturing to America, new policies to stop or stem the in-flow of immigrants, legal or illegal, and eliminating the competition for jobs between immigrants and native-born Americans.

National Populism reject the opportunity state where people are self-reliant and rise through hard work in a free market economy. In the National Populist view, only government intervention allows individuals to succeed. Steve Bannon, former Trump strategist, explained, *"Like [Andrew] Jackson's populism, we're going to build an entirely new political movement.... It's everything related to jobs. The conservatives are going to go crazy. I'm the guy pushing a trillion-dollar infrastructure plan. With negative interest rates throughout the world, it's the greatest opportunity to rebuild everything. Shipyards, iron works, get them all jacked up. We're just going to throw it up against the wall and see if it sticks. It will be as exciting as the 1930s, greater than the Reagan revolution — conservatives, plus populists, in an economic nationalist movement."4*

Trump, for his occasional talk about conservative ideas, often turned back to his liberal views throughout the election cycle when he got into trouble or looked for answers when stumped. During the Wisconsin primary, he attacked Scott Walker's reforms from the left as he stated that Walker should have surrendered to the unions and raised taxes. He simply recited leftist talking points—and this was not the first time in this election that he would resort to leftist talking points.

Trump may have conservative ideas but unlike Bernie Sanders, he has no strongly held beliefs and what he believes today, he will change tomorrow, or even within an hour depending upon the circumstance. Trump has been consistent on *one* view: trade policy and protectionism. He is not just building a wall to keep out illegal immigrants; he is building a trade wall to keep out foreign goods. His attacks on Wall Street and companies that move factories overseas are no different than those of Bernie Sanders. Over the past twenty years, Trump's views throughout the past two decades have included many leftist ideas: taxing the rich, single payer health care, gun controls, pro-abortion positions. Trump is not conservative and before he ran, was not really a Republican (even though in the eyes of his supporters this proved a benefit). The main concern is that National Populism threatens to tear apart what remains of the American Creed.

I got into a Twitter exchange with an individual who actually defended fascism when he tweeted out brilliant thoughts like, *"And fascism is bad* *why exactly?...I would like to hear your input on why fascism is bad. I feel the word Nazi might be involved...and more often than not fascism needs to be supported by a nationalistic populism. But nationalist doesn't = racist...capitalism allows the rich to get grossly richer and the poor to pay for the poor... all profits from these corps are put into social programs and welfare. Unlike the tax based system we have now...<u>corporations in a fascist state are ALLOWED to exist only for the sole purpose of benefiting the public.</u>"*

Let these words sink in, and understand what they really mean.

In a free economy, business benefit the public by providing people with goods and services and paying wages and benefits to employees. The public rewards the owners of a business with profit for providing value to customers. Companies that do not provide value quickly disappear.

In the National Populist and Democratic Socialist worldview, the value businesses provide is not determined by individual consumers but by the government. In the American Creed, the individual predicates success. In National Populism and Democratic Socialism, success is dictated and delivered by the state.

After another four or eight years of flat wages and political disappointment, the supporters of National Populism and Democratic Socialism could form a new economic coalition based on protectionism, limited immigration, income redistribution and government support for preferred industries. This could happen easier than many suspects because National Populism is the mirror image of Democratic Socialism.

The only different is that Trump will use government to benefit *his* supporters and business associates as opposed to those companies that Bernie Sanders and Hillary Clinton would've supported. The conference room bargaining would be over which group of corporate cronies gets the spoils. Examining Democratic Socialism in detail shows just how easily it could merge with National Populism.

Who Is Donald Trump?

In 1929, Herbert Hoover became President. Before being president, Herbert Hoover's reputation was that of a self-made millionaire and brilliant manager. He served as Secretary of Commerce under the Harding and Coolidge administrations and to many voters he was the Great Engineer who would bring all of his business expertise to government. While much of Hoover's reputation was that of a conservative, the reality was that Hoover was a progressive Republican. My father once reminded me that much of the New Deal began under Herbert Hoover and his run for President in 1928 emphasized his business expertise and his managerial skills, which included his efforts in heading the American Relief Administration, which relieved the hunger of more than 200 million people from 1914 through 1922.

Hoover was a disciple of the Efficiency Movement, which sought to eliminate waste throughout the economy and society. This movement played an essential role in the Progressive era in the United States. The theory began that society and government would be better if experts fixed national problems once they were identified. Hoover felt comfortable with the Progressive movement. I bring Hoover up since Trump's campaign is similar to the Hoover appeal—a businessman who will run government by bringing in the best experts. *Trump doesn't talk about "reducing the size and role of government" but talks of managing the present government better.*

In her biography, *Herbert Hoover: Forgotten Progressive*, author Joan Hoff Wilson described Hoover's economic thinking:

"The version of Hoover presented in the media's narrative of Hoover as champion of laissez faire bears little resemblance to the details of Hoover's life, the ideas he held, and the policies he adopted as president. Where the classical economists like Adam Smith had argued for uncontrolled competition between independent economic units guided only by the invisible hand of supply and

demand, he talked about voluntary national economic planning arising from cooperation between business interests and the government.....Instead of negative government action in times of depression, he advocated the expansion of public works, avoidance of wage cuts, increased rather than decreased production—measures that would expand rather than contract purchasing power." [5]

St. Lawrence University economist Steve Horwitz added, *"Hoover was also a long-time critic of international free trade, and favored increased inheritance taxes, public dams, and, significantly, government regulation of the stock market. This was not the program of a devotee of laissez faire, and he was determined to use the Commerce Department to implement it."* [6] Trump, like Hoover, opposes international free trade and in the past talked of surtaxes on the rich. The similarity between the progressive Hoover and the progressive Trump is eerie.

Trump's model of Republicanism will be similar to Hoover's and Richard Nixon's. Nixon was a statist as president including creating new bureaucracies like the Occupational Health and Safety Administration and the Environmental Protection Agency as well as instituting wage and price controls. Nixon's goal was to make government work for the middle class and his supporters—*his silent majority.*

Trump, like Hoover, is a protectionist who believes in a managerial approach to governing. Hoover dealt with the Great Depression by raising taxes to nearly triple the previous marginal rate. He increased government spending and his tariffs, along with the higher taxes, led to a spiraling economic descent. He helped turn a recession into the Great Depression.

Richard Nixon's own economic policies, along with the paralysis of the Watergate scandal, led to the stagflation of the 1970s, which included slow or no growth along with high inflation at the end of the decade under Jimmy Carter. It wasn't until the Reagan years that the back of inflation was broken. After, we saw more than two decades of economic growth resulting in a rise of income for the middle class that continued during the Clinton administration.

The occasional autarky policies including his protectionist planks proposed by Trump will not enhance the lives of those who support him, just as Hoover's policies failed to improve the life of the average American. At a time when international trade is retrenching, Trump's protectionism could lead to a recession since his entire economic strategy is to build a wall to keep out foreign goods. Considering that Bernie Sanders's ideas on trade are similar, Trump or Sanders's policies could lead to as sharp as an economic decline as Herbert Hoover's.

(As for trade and imposing tariffs, we will discuss the historical record of trade in the United States later in this book and we don't know what Trump trade policies will end up. If Trump lowers taxes and keep government spending under control while not jacking tariffs too high; the tariffs may not harm the economy and the United States will grow. *Hoover's mistake was that he not only raised tariffs, but also increased government spending and raised taxes.*)

While Trump is like Hoover and Nixon, he is quite different than Reagan. <u>*While many Trump supporters try to compare their guy to Reagan*</u> throughout the 2016 election, there are significant differences. Unlike Trump and Hoover, Reagan was an accomplished politician who had been on the political scene for two decades. Before that, he was a well-known actor.

Before Reagan became president, he had been fighting for conservative ideals for three decades and understood the political process as well as the ideas behind them. Kiron Skinner, Annelise Anderson and the late Martin Anderson's own research confirmed his substantive knowledge of the issues by reviewing and publishing many of his diaries and other private writings.

In 1967, Reagan was invited to be part of a debate with Robert F Kennedy on American foreign policy and destroyed him and eleven years later, he won a debate with Bill Buckley on the Panama Canal. These two debates showed he had the ability to go toe to toe with some of the best debaters of his era.

There is one similarity between Ronald Reagan and Donald Trump is that both were consistently underrated. Trump in 2016 as debater succeeded with his attitude, not on what he knew. The four words, "Make America Great Again," exhibits Trump's mindset. He wants to reverse the decline he sees. Trump may prove to be more of an experimenter than following a set game plan, seeking what works. Another similarity with Reagan and Trump is that both reached blue-collar workers. In 1980, these voters were called Reagan Democrats. Now they are called Trump Republicans.

How often have we heard what a great dealmaker Trump is? How many people will remember that Reagan was the master of negotiations? When Trump, during the election, made the case that Reagan worked with Tip O'Neill, he did not remember Reagan did not deal with Tip O'Neill, *he dealt against O'Neill* by working with moderate Democrats to get much of his budget and tax policies passed. Reagan had a Democratic majority in the House plus heavy opposition in the Senate. Many moderate Republicans were against his economic plans and he did not deal with O'Neill. Instead, he dealt with many of the moderate and conservative Democrats and went around O'Neill. Trump has a Republican Congress but one lesson from the Reagan years is that Trump needs to go over the heads of the leftist Democrats who oppose him.

Reagan's deal-making with the Russians was exemplary, but Reagan's success is that he dealt from strength. The Nuclear Freeze was in full force during his first administration as the left were trying to keep America from putting Pershing missiles into Europe to counter the Soviet SS-20 and undermine his military buildup. His first goal was to rebuild the military before dealing with the Russians and to wait for the right moment. That moment did not come until Mikhail Gorbachev took over the Soviet Empire in 1985 during his second term. Reagan negotiated the removal of intermediate-range nuclear missiles in both Europe and Russia in 1987 because the year before, he walked out of the Reykjavik conference on nuclear arms reduction. Reagan's policy set the stage for the collapse of the Soviet Union.

Reagan walked into the White House with a worldview and a plan to go with that worldview. Unlike Reagan, Trump does not have a history of consistent ideology. While some view this as a plus and the start of new era of no ideology, Trump is not an ideologue and this is shown in his cabinet appointments as he selected conservatives like Rick Perry and Scott Pruitt but others such as Steve Mnuchin are outsiders. Trump appointments come from all factions of the Republican Party and, in the case of Mnuchin, a political novice with no public record as a political activist other than his donations, most given to Democrats. Trump's ideology is based on Trump the man and brand divorced from a consistent worldview. While Reagan began his career as a Democrat, his move to the right aligned with his movement toward traditional Republican values. The jury is still out on Trump.

Throughout the election Trump's two signature issues were immigration and trade. He has exploited the yawning gap between the views of the elites in both parties and the public on these issues. He feasted on the public discontent over a government that can't be bothered to enforce its own laws on immigration no matter how many times it says it will.

A few short years ago, Trump was criticizing Mitt Romney for having the temerity to propose "self-deportation," or the entirely reasonable policy of reducing the illegal population through attrition while enforcing the nation's laws. By time the 2016 election began, Trump did a 180-degree turn as he pledged to deport 11 million illegals here in the United States, a colossal administrative and logistical task not beyond the capacity of the federal government, but certainly an expensive proposition that would rupture any chance of capturing a significant percentage of Hispanic voters in the future. Trump tried to have it both ways by proposing a "touchback" provision and declaring that he would allow many of the illegal immigrants to return to the U.S. once they had been deported, which makes his policy a poorly disguised amnesty (and a version of ideas already proposed as part of Washington's episodic "comprehensive" immigration reforms during the George W. Bush Administration.) As Marc A. Thiessen of the American Enterprise Institute observed, the "touchback" provision actually came from moderate Republican senator Kay Bailey Hutchison.[7]

The result of his proposals will be similar to others; that vast majority of those here illegally will still be here after his reform. The question is will he actually do a touchback and deport 11 million illegals only to bring them back? His own past history suggests otherwise.

As *National Review* published their dissent over Trump in December 2015, Trump got valuable support from the Iowa Republican establishment based on his support for ethanol while they opposed Cruz due to Cruz's opposition toward ethanol. The Iowa GOP establishment made it clear they preferred Trump to Cruz to protect their own subsidies.

The Republican primary in Iowa was between the ghost of Richard Nixon and the spirit of Ronald Reagan with Trump playing Nixon while Rubio and Cruz represented what was left of the spirit of Reagan. Nixon ran in 1968 on behalf of the silent majority who were overtaxed, whose sons were fighting in Vietnam, and who witnessed crime going up. Nixon ran a law-and-order campaign and when he governed, he expanded the welfare state in his first term while giving us the EPA. His goal was to rein in the bureaucratic state and create a conservative big government that worked for the middle class. He did not reduce government spending or power. Like Nixon, Trump ran on a law and order platform, including standing up for a new generation of forgotten Americans, many of whom fought in Afghanistan and Iraq.

Trump appeared in front of the "non-partisan" group No Labels before the New Hampshire primary. The No Labels group desperately wanted candidates who would "compromise" even though it is never clear what policies would result from these compromises. Donald Trump told this group:

"Let me just tell you, the word compromise is not a bad word to me. I like the word compromise. We need compromise, there is nothing wrong with compromise, but it's always good to compromise and win. Meaning, let's compromise and win." [8]

Reporter Byron York's thesis from observing Trump is that Trump's prone to saying the outrageous thing or begins with the outrageous position so he can get what he wants. This is Trump the dealmaker who understands you won't get all what you want so you start with many positions that you know you can throw away to negotiate.

Let's return to Trump's ideas on immigration. As Trump told CNN's Dana Bash:

"I would get people out and then have an expedited way of getting them back into the country so they can be legal.... A lot of these people are helping us...and sometimes it's jobs a citizen of the United States doesn't want to do. I want to move 'em out, and we're going to move 'em back in and let them be legal." [9]

Would this be any different than the policies of a President Rubio or a President Jeb Bush?

Whil e it is hard to know if Trump truly understand fully what his political agenda, it's clear that but many of his supporters do. Ann Coulter has made it clear that for her, the litmus test is immigration restrictions starting with building the wall and deportation. Her political strategy is what a black conservative friend of mine, Vernon Robinson, called, "the search for one more white voter." In an era in which Hispanics and Asians are playing greater roles in battleground states, Coulter doesn't believe that Republicans can make inroads within the minority communities and wants the GOP to double down on white voter outreach.

While Coulter is correct that the GOP can't outbid the Democrats on the immigration issue, they can succeed in getting enough minorities to win key battleground states by emphasizing other issues. To have a strategy simply to increase the number of white voters at the polls is a losing proposition in the long term. The last time Republicans won more than 60 percent of the white voters in the past forty years was the 1984 election in which Reagan won 64 percent. Many Republicans in 2014 managed to get enough minority voters like Cory Gardner did to win Colorado. (Gardner in his Senate race in Colorado and Scott Walker in Wisconsin actually underperformed among white voters than the GOP nationally but got enough of the Democratic base including minorities to win.) In 2004, Bush did receive 40 percent of Hispanic voters, which aided his victory over John Kerry.

I am not opposed to increasing white voter turnout and many of our ad campaign over the past two years have done that. As we will discuss later in this book, both Ron Johnson and Rod Blum went after white voters but Ron Johnson also campaigned in the minority communities. One can simultaneously add additional blue-collar white voters and many minority voters who agree with our agenda. Trump gained enough minorities in key battleground states to ensure victory. Trump's campaign simultaneously tried to increase white voters while getting enough minorities to win. It appears that he will design policies to attract minorities.

The real issue is this: how do we build a new conservative majority? Ann Coulter's view is to drive up white voter turnout and worry less about appealing to minorities. Others are attempting to preach conservative values to expand minority support for conservative ideas. Trump's success is that he speaks to the guy or gal who sits at the end of the bar every day and whose life is not working. They drink to forget that their income is stagnant and bemoan a future that looks bleaker by the day. The question that remains is: how do we reach that guy and move the conservative movement forward? How do we promote a liberty agenda? Can a man who spent his life as a crony capitalist be trusted with that liberty agenda and fight crony capitalism that supports the political class?

Democratic Socialism

I n Sanders's worldview, there is no mention of creating wealth or expanding opportunity for the middle class.

As *National Review*'s Kevin Williamson noted, "*Sanders worldview
begins with the idea there are just too few people, the 1 percent, who have far
too much wealth and this wealth has allowed the Rich the tilt the economy in
their favor. Sanders believes in a zero sum economics in which wealth is not
created but needs to be shared equally.*"

Bernie Sanders's view of trade and immigration is not much different
from Trump as he told the editorial board of the *New York Daily News*
when he stated that he agreed with Trump that we negotiated bad trade
deals, and added, "*I do believe in trade. But it has to be based on principles
that are fair. So if you are in Vietnam, where the minimum wage is 65 cents
an hour, you're in Malaysia, where many of the workers are indentured
servants because their passports are taken away when come into this country
and are working in slave-like conditions, no, I'm not going to have American
workers 'competing' against you under those conditions. So you have to have
standards. And what fair trade means to say that it is fair. It is roughly
equivalent to the wages and environmental standards in the United States...I
don't think it is appropriate for trade policies to say that you can move to a
country where wages are abysmal, where are no environmental regulations,
where workers can't form unions. That's not the kind of trade agreement that
I will support.*" [10]

Sanders is making the case that he wants no trade with emerging econ-
omies. But what if trade is an important vehicle to lift these countries out
of poverty? Note these countries are either Asian or Hispanics dominated,
so Sanders opposes trade with countries with people of color not white.

In the journal *Democracy: Journal of Ideas*, a symposium featuring,
"The Middle-Out Moment," discusses on how the left view the economy

today. Eric Liu and Nick Hanauer note, *"Middle-out economics argues that national prosperity does not trickle down from wealthy business people or corporations; rather, it flows in a virtuous cycle that starts with a thriving middle class. Middle-out economics demands a systemic policy focus on the skills, capacities, and income of the middle class."*[11] Investment and capital formation are not mentioned, but for Elizabeth Warren, Barack Obama, and Hillary Clinton, give money to the middle class and magically wealth is created. The question of where we get the money before giving it to the middle class is never discussed. As Liu and Hanauer write, *"Demand from the middle class- not tax cuts for the wealthy- is what drives a virtuous cycle and job growth and prosperity…Rich businesspeople are not the primary job creators, middle-class customers are; the more the middle class can buy, the more jobs we'll create…Middle-out economics means investing in the health, education, infrastructure, and purchasing power of the middle class."*[12] This is the essential aspect of democratic socialism—provide the Middle Class with benefits and money from the government and multipliers will kick in with the growing economy.

What is missing from this formula is the *creation* of wealth. How often during the 2012 election did we hear from Obama or Senator Warren that entrepreneurs didn't build their business but government did through the creation of roads and schools; entrepreneurs and business merely were inventions of government policies as oppose to being created by entrepreneurs themselves. Businesses, say the democratic socialists, are to be servant of the government, contributing to what the government deems necessary.

Sanders stated during this election, *"You can't just continue growth for the sake of growth in a world in which we are struggling with climate change and all kinds of environmental problems. All right? You don't necessarily need a choice of 23 underarm spray deodorants or of 18 different pairs of sneakers when children are hungry in this country. I don't think the media appreciates the kind of stress that ordinary Americans are working on."*[13] For Sanders, all of economics is a zero-sum game in which a producer of underarm deodorants are stealing food from hungry children and government must step in to guide businesses in the right direction while taking from the wealthy to share with the Middle Class and the poor.

While Sanders talks mostly about class, the machinery of the Democratic Party is built on activists, public sector unions, along with upper income consultants who benefit from government largess and are funded by leftist oligarchs.

Who Benefits from Democratic Socialism and National Populism?

For Democratic Socialism, the beneficiaries are public sector unions who benefit from the growth of government (and possible bailouts when pension plans in blue states like Illinois go belly up), selected IT companies like Apple and Google who are big contributors, Green "tech companies" and, special interest groups just as various grassroots like Black Lives Matter who help bring in the ground troops for election get out the vote drives and those on Wall Street who allied themselves with Democratic socialists.

For National Populism, the beneficiaries are less defined but it begins with those who benefit from protectionism, including established businesses. Those that don't benefit will be those companies such as Apple or Ford who move factories abroad or who allied themselves with the opposition. Trump favored bailouts of both Wall Street and the auto industries so his bias will be those business that he is familiar with or "manufacturing companies" like General Motors that he favors. It is less about ideology with Trumpism and more about "who is on my side," similar to the corporations who benefited from Mussolini in the 1920s and 1930s. Contrast Trump, who has spent his political resources on those politicians that benefited him to the Koch brothers, who have taken stances that even hurt their own bottom line due to their consistent free market philosophy. In many ways Trump is a disciple of John Kenneth Galbraith's theory that big business, big labor, and activist government manage the economy and Trump views himself the guy who can manage it all. Trump also favors massive investment in infrastructure, which goes with supporting blue-collar workers through government largess.

For the Democratic Socialists, those businesses and groups that benefit from bigger government and National Populism is more about finding businesses that will fund government's efforts and whose contributions guarantee their inclusion at the table. These companies tend to be older and established businesses needing protection from competition.

On immigration, both Sanders and Trump view immigrants as cheap labor for major corporations. But there is a divide among Democratic Socialists since there is a belief that the more illegals there are in the US, the more votes for Democrats, whereas National Populists view immigrants as competing for jobs with many lower income blue collar workers, most of them white.

Trump views immigrants as he does trade—as people who are screwing American workers. For many of Trump's supporters, immigrants are competing against their jobs, and while most of Trump's voters are not racists or fascists there is no doubt that there is a racist virus, known as the "alt-right," that exists within the National Populist movement. The "alt-right" are neither conservatives nor part of the right.

Both Trump and Sanders make it clear that they will not reform entitlements. But many of Trump's supporters view welfare as a sop for the poor. On healthcare issues, Sanders is consistent in his support for single payer. Trump is all over the map with supporting free-market reforms and repealing Obamacare but ensuring that the poor will be given free healthcare. In the past, Trump has praised Canadian and European single payer systems. Trump's stances on negotiating drug prices is an attempt to reduce drug prices for the blue-collar workers in his base, while attacking big Pharmaceutical companies, many of whom made deals with the Obama administration to save their profitability.

Sanders and his movement view regulations as needed to control business to ensure that workers "are protected." Trump's view on business regulation is less defined but Trump's own view of regulation presently is to reduce the regulatory drag on the economy that affects his own base, in particular the fossil fuel industries.

National Populism and Democratic Socialism tell the same story with variations on the victim, villain and hero. Socialism has always been about a narrative and Trump is just a natural at creating a narrative that resonates. Whites with traditional middle-class values prefer national Populism while whites with a progressive bent prefer Democratic Socialism. Left out of the mix are blacks, Hispanics, and Asians. For many blacks and

Hispanics, they have not only seen their own income drop but Democratic Socialists have created barriers that will ensure they stay at the bottom of the economic ladder, such as supporting education policies that see many minorities trapped in inferior public schools from which many white progressives can and do escape from by going to private schools. Education policies hurt minorities from moving up economically as they fail to get the knowledge needed for advancement. Many Asians have been economically successful as a group compared to blacks, Hispanics, and even whites but many of the affirmative action programs enforced at many colleges target them more as a group than even whites.

Blacks and Hispanics are expected to provide voting margins to the Democratic Socialists while Republicans compete for the majority of white voters. Trump's margin among blue-collar votes was higher than Romney's in 2012 but he ran behind Romney among white, college-educated voters and even lost white, college-educated women. As we discuss later, Trump did not expand the Republican or conservative coalition. The margin that minorities provide the Democratic Socialists could allow them the ability to keep power possibility for the next generation beyond 2018, especially if the Democrats find a way to increase their numbers among white voters. Even though the vast majority of Hispanics and blacks don't benefit economically from Democratic Socialism there is little reason right now for a Hispanic or black voter to view National Populism granting them any additional benefits.

What do conservatives need to do to build a new majority? As we will show, much of Trump's margin in many key battleground states came from not just an increase of White blue-collar votes but also the number of black additional votes for Trump compared to Romney and the number of black voters staying home instead of voting for Hillary Clinton. Trump has opened the door for Republican inroads into the minority communities. Will the Republicans move through the door?

The Democratic War on Freedom

The Left's Stalinist tactics were on full display when Loretta Lynch confirmed in the summer of 2016 she was referring complaints to the Justice Department against oil companies for potential criminal prosecution. Senator Sheldon Whitehouse, a leading Democratic climate alarmist, had one goal to jail oil company executives who disagree with his theories on how humans are destroying mankind and bankrupt the fossil fuel companies. As *Power Line*'s John Hinderaker noted, *"The Obama Administration's idea of a crime is not, apparently, violating federal laws and regulations and State Department procedures in a manner that exposes thousands of classified documents to our enemies. No, that isn't the sort of conduct that is likely to draw an indictment from Loretta Lynch's Department of Justice. Obama's DOJ is more interested in trying to jail scientists who point out the rather obvious flaws in the government's desperate effort to convince Americans that global warming is our greatest threat."* [14]

The Obama administration and Democratic Senators were not just politicizing science but they were enforcing their scientific worldview. They looked to the justice department and government bureaucracies to destroy fossil fuels and criminalize scientific difference. As John Hinderaker observed:

"The Soviets did that, in order to shore up the hopeless but government-favored theories of Lysenko. Until now, such conduct would have been unthinkable in an American administration. But Barack Obama, to his everlasting shame, is willing to emulate Josef Stalin by threatening criminal prosecution of those who disagree with the equally hopeless theories of Michael Mann et al. American history has come to a very sad pass." [15]

While many view Donald Trump being a fascist, just remember which political party used legal action against opponents, including using the IRS to go after conservative groups; having local Democrat prosecutors

21

use Gestapo tactics to go after Scott Walker's supporters in Wisconsin; and now, threatening to use racketeering laws against climate realists who don't agree with the conventional wisdom that human activity is the key reason for climate change. So who are the fascists, the Stalinists?

Meanwhile, the skeptics' worldview keeps being proven correct. I need to remind the reader that scientists whether they are skeptics or alarmists, there is a general consensus that climate is changing. The skeptic worldview notes the historical record that climate change has been occurring since the planet was formed and there are skeptics who don't discount human involvement but temper it with the effects of nature and that human activity may not all that damaging. Some scientists are crediting the rise of carbon dioxide levels with enhancing plant life and aiding in increased agricultural output. The alarmists view humans as the cause of modern day climate change and don't even acknowledge or consider that natural events play a role.

The alarmists' attempt to manipulate science is being challenged and in Trump's administration, climate skeptics and climate realists will get the hearing they earned. The government announcement last year that they have proven the pause in climate temperature since 1998 didn't exist was deflated by another study that proved what climate realists have stated all along; we are in the midst of pause in climate temperature change. From *Nature*, *"But in June last year, a study in* Science *claimed that the hiatus was just an artifact, which vanishes when biases in temperature data are corrected. Now a prominent group of researchers is countering that claim, arguing in* Nature Climate Change *that even after correcting these biases the slowdown was real. 'There is this mismatch between what the climate models are producing and what the observations are showing,' says lead author John Fyfe, a climate modeler at the Canadian Centre for Climate Modelling and Analysis in Victoria, British Columbia. 'We can't ignore it.'"*[16] It should be pointed out that many of these researchers were considered climate alarmists and it showed that science is not settled which makes the efforts of Senator Whitehouse and others even more alarming since their own science is under siege.

The government is going after fossil fuel companies while the EPA is doing its best to destroy the coal industry and those high paying jobs that go with them. Power Line's John Hinderaker wrote:

"Actually, the oil companies have mostly been bystanders in the climate debate. But the Democrats are trying to deflect attention away from the fact that their global warming theory is crumbling in the face of the facts. The oil companies make convenient scapegoats...What is outrageous about this is not the debate—no matter however flimsy, dishonest and self-interested the government-funded alarmists may be—but rather the Democrats' attempt to shut the debate off by trying to imprison those who won't toe their line. This is the most blatant violation of the First Amendment that we have seen in a very long time." [17]

The Democratic Party has become the enemy of scientific research and free speech, as they are attempting to stop the exchange of ideas and ensure that their ideas are what triumph.

Recently *The New York Times* detailed a whole story on Trump's media attack. While much of the criticism in the article is valid including Trump's own veiled threat against press freedom of speech, *The New York Times* has been missing in action when similar attacks by the left on political free speech and the tactics that have been used to silence Trump and others.

In California, there were legislators attempting to criminalize anyone who disagree with the notion that humans are the root cause of present climate change. Senate Bill 1161 or the California Climate Science Truth Accountability Act of 2016, would have allowed prosecutors to sue fossil fuel companies and think tanks who by their estimate, *"deceived or misled the public on the risk of climate change."* [18] The bill never made it out of committee, and was not considered by the California Senate.

This is part of a broader effort to punish fossil fuels companies and think tanks to ensure uniform opinion on climate change and brook no dissent. It is as if the left seems to ignore the First Amendment or even understand the scientific process where the truth can be elusive. For every answer, sometimes more questions are raised. The left over the years has used the government including the IRS to attack conservative groups with the goal of intimidation.

It has been recognized that we have seen a hiatus in temperature rise over the past two decades but some climate alarmists extremists are now using their usual cherry picking of data to prove the hiatus never happened and could be eliminated by looking at the data in a new way. The problem is that climate alarmist in Britain have stated that climate realists are right, the hiatus is real. So the "settled science" is not really settled as alarmists can't even agree on what is going on with their own computer models.

There have been a thousand studies over the past three years alone challenging the climate alarmists' worldview, and showing that the science of climate change is far from being fully understood. This may explain why many alarmists and their allies in Congress and the media wants the debate shut down.

A report from *Insurance Journal* noted that dealing with global warming is more than a $1.5 trillion a year global business. In 2011, money spent fighting global warming—consulting, renewables, green buildings, hybrid vehicles—increased 15 percent after a decade of solid growth. That doesn't include the billions of government research dollars directed to researchers, many of whom allied themselves with alarmists.

The companies owned by the Koch brothers have revenues that are a tenth of that spent on green technology. To keep those government contracts going, green technology companies have been major contributors to the Democratic Party. It's far from clear that these grants are helpful or do much more than subsidize activists.

Some climate scientists have called for federal funds to be cut off because the field is too ideological. MIT scientist Richard Lindzen noted, *"Even in 1990 no one at MIT called themselves a 'climate scientist,' and then all of a sudden everyone was. They only entered it because of the bucks; they realized it was a gravy train. You have to get it back to the people who only care about the science…They should probably cut the funding by 80 to 90 percent until the field cleans up, Climate science has been set back two generations, and they have destroyed its intellectual foundations."*

Twenty scientists, led by Jagadish Shukla of George Mason University signed a petition to have the government prosecute "climate skeptics and deniers" with the RICO act. The petition was withdrawn, but Shukla continues to be investigated as to how he could run a green research institute part-time while simultaneously being a full-time professor at George Mason, a possible violation of Virginia state law that prohibits professors from moonlighting on the job.[19]

The witch hunt led by environmentalists is part of the larger witch hunt by the left in their effort to silence or intimidate conservatives.

Consider the case of Donald Trump's rallies, where the goal of rioters was to stop Trump from speaking and to intimidate his supporters with the threat of violence. The rioters' view, since Trump was a fascist, was it was okay to break the law and threaten his supporters. While Trump was my 17th favorite candidate out of the 17 that ran in 2016, but he has as much right to speak without intimidation as you or I. The left is already stifling free speech whether it is keeping conservative speakers from speaking at college campuses including the threat of violence using the IRS to target conservative groups, using goon squads to intimidate Republican candidate supporters or threatening those they disagree with jail time.

The left's interference with Trump rallies during the 2016 primary season resulted in violence in San Jose. After the San Jose riot, the Democratic mayor failed to blame the rioters, but instead blamed the Trump campaign. Nor has this been the first violence at a Trump rally. A week earlier, 18 people were injured and 35 people arrested at a San Diego rally and in another violent incident in Costa Mesa two months before that, crowds smashed the windows of a police car and tried to flip it over. During the Illinois primary, hooligans shut down a Trump rally. Democratic activists Robert Creamer and Scott Foval admitted that they trained operatives to cause incite violence at Trump's rallies and there is solid evidence that members of the Democratic National Committee not only knew this was occurring but supported it. These efforts were part of an effort to intimidate Republican and conservative voters repeated over the previous eight years.

In Wisconsin, the left's efforts to silence the right resulted in a partisan witch-hunt against supporters of Republican Gov. Scott Walker. While supposedly enforcing campaign regulations, Milwaukee County Democratic prosecutor John Chisholm used campaign finance laws in a cynical war against conservative organizations in the state. Local law enforcement used flood lights in their victims' front yards, and armed officers seized documents, computers, cellphones, and other devices.

Chisholm was conducting a "John Doe investigation" of which the targets of the investigation were barred from talking about it. Eric O' Keefe, director of the Wisconsin Club for Growth, violated the gag order and openly spoke out against the war waged against him by the Democrats and decided he would stand in his way of the Democratic manipulation of Wisconsin campaign laws. Judge Rudolph Randa, hearing O'Keefe's horror stories, halted the Democratic corruption. In 2015, the Wisconsin Supreme Court ruled that Chisholm had no case and O'Keefe and other conservatives were innocent.

Just read how Judge Rudolph Randa described the "John Doe investigation," *"Early in the morning of October 3, 2013, armed officers raided the homes of R.J. Johnson, WCFG (Wisconsin Club for Growth) advisor Deborah Jordahl, and several other targets across the state. ECF No. 5-15, O'Keefe Declaration, Sheriff Deputy Vehicles used bright floodlights to illuminate the targets' homes. Deputies executed the search warrants, seizing business papers, computer equipment, phones, and other devices, while their targets were restrained under police supervision and denied the ability to contact their attorneys. Among the materials seized were many of the Club's records that were in the possession of Ms. Jordahl and Mr. Johnson. The warrants indicate that they were executed at the request of GAB investigator Dean Nickel.*

On the same day, the Club's accountants and directors, including O'Keefe, received subpoenas demanding that they turn over more or less all of the Club's records from March 1, 2009 to the present. The subpoenas indicated that their recipients were subject to a Secrecy Order, and that their contents and existence could not be disclosed other than to counsel, under penalty of perjury. The subpoenas' list of advocacy groups indicates that all or nearly all right-of-center groups and individuals in Wisconsin who engaged in issue advocacy from 2010 to the present are targets of the investigation…The defendants are pursuing criminal charges through a secret John Doe investigation against the plaintiffs for exercising issue advocacy speech rights that on their face are not subject to the regulations or statutes the defendants seek to enforce. This legitimate exercise of O'Keefe's rights as an individual, and WCFG's rights as a 501(c)(4) corporation, to speak on the issues has been characterized by the defendants as political activity covered by Chapter 11 of the Wisconsin Statutes, rendering the plaintiffs a subcommittee of the Friends of Scott Walker and requiring that money spent on such speech be reported as an in-kind campaign contribution. This interpretation is simply wrong." [20]

This was a blatant attempt by Democrats to shut down conservative organizations in Wisconsin. It is yet another example of the left war against free speech.

How Many Illegals Vote?

Still another example of liberal manipulation is on Election Day. Consider the number of illegal aliens who vote.

The number of non-citizens voting across the United States is a major problem. Jess Richman and David Earnest of Old Dominion University reviewed incidents of voting by non-citizens and while some have argued that this is inconsequential, Richman and Earnest attempted to find exactly how many non-citizens vote. Richman and Earnest concluded, "Most non-citizens do not register, let alone vote. *But enough do that their participation can change the outcome of close races.*"[21]

Using data from the Cooperative Congressional Election Study, they attempted to find out how many non-citizens voted. They found that 14 percent non-citizens of both 2008 and 2010 samples were registered to vote and they estimated that 6.5 percent of non-citizens voted in 2008 and 2.2 percent voted in 2010.

Their estimation that based on CCES samples that Obama won 80 percent of non-citizens' votes and while this did not affect the general election, they viewed that it could have account for some Democratic victories in Senate races, including Al Franken's victory over Norm Coleman in 2008. Franken's margin was 312 votes and as they concluded, "Votes cast by just .65 percent of Minnesota non-citizens could account for this margin. It is also possible that non-citizen votes were responsible for Obama's 14,177 votes, so a turnout by 5.1 percent of North Carolina adult non-citizens would have provided the margin" for Obama's victory in North Carolina. Richman and Earnest noted that three-quarters of non-citizens had photo IDs when asked to provide them.

Virginia Republican activist William Campenni, writing in *Power Line*, observed, *"For years here in Virginia I have observed massive fraud — in the registration process, in the absentee ballot casting, in the battle to remove photo IDs, in the voting at the polls. Recent studies have shown thousands of illegal alien registrations in Virginia, and hundreds of voters also casting votes in other states (college kids the worst offenders). My own identity (SS No.) was stolen last year and used to get a fraudulent tax refund and voting…For over a decade the SEIU and its local affiliates have gone through the extensive illegal alien community here in Virginia fraudulently registering illegals who then vote in large numbers, usually in early voting or absentee ballots, because there are no poll watchers to challenge them. They even brag about it."* [22]

He added that the incumbent Republican George Allen may have lost to Jim Webb in 2006 because of illegal voters and present Governor Terry McAuliffe may have won his seats due to it. He concluded, "(Mark) Warner defeated Ed Gillespie for Senate in 2014 by a small vote difference provided by illegals. And my friend the local former Fairfax County Democrat head brags about it when we have coffee together.'"

Former Department of Justice J. Christian Adams mention a result of study conducted by Public Interest Legal Foundation looking onto small number of Virginia Counties found that 1,000 were removed from the rolls due to citizenship problems and at least 200 of these individuals voted. Adams quoted Democratic operative John Podesta in emails disclosed by *WikiLeaks*: *"Podesta seems to have figured out that, because of vulnerabilities in our election system, **foreigners can get registered to vote and get voter ID at the same time.** Podesta's right, and has revealed one of the biggest vulnerabilities in American elections, all because of the Motor Voter law."* [23] Only four states attempt to determine the citizenship of people obtaining driver's licenses. Three of them are entangled in ligation. As Richman and Earnest noted, 80 percent of non-citizens voted for Obama in 2008 and others just as a Pew Research Center survey estimated that those non-citizens who identify with a political party, do so at a three-to-one ratio in favor of Democrats. .

Americas Majority Foundation, as part of a post-election survey, asked voters if they were U.S. citizens or not. The results of the study showed that a small but significant percentage of the voting population self-reported they were not U.S. citizens. (Our methodology was a simple self-reporting system in which voters were asked if they were U.S. citizens; some voters did admit they were not U.S. citizens.)

We conducted two national polls with two different pollsters with Voice Broadcasting poll showed that 2.1 percent of the population who voted were not U.S. citizen and the second national poll had the numbers at .9 percent. While this may not sound like a lot, we are talking anywhere from 1,200,000 to 2,800,000 voters nationwide.

This alone could have added anywhere from 580,000 popular votes to slightly more than 1,330,000 votes to Hillary Clinton's total. (This was based on Democrat candidates receiving 75 percent of non-citizens' votes, which may be a conservative estimate. If Richman and Earnest are right about the number of illegals voting Democrat being 80 percent or higher, these estimates are probably low.)

This question was asked of 34,000 plus voters in seven states: Nevada, Colorado, Wisconsin, Michigan, Pennsylvania, Ohio, and North Carolina. The breakdown was as following of non-citizen voting: 2.3 percent in Nevada, 1.8 percent in Colorado, 3.8 percent in Wisconsin, 2.5 percent in Michigan, 2.1 percent in Ohio, 2.4 percent in Pennsylvania.

While this did not affect the outcome of the presidential or senatorial races in those states there is no doubt that illegal alien votes decreased the percentage of voters who were Republican and increased those of Democrats. We estimate that Democrats received a boost of at least 19,000 votes in Nevada, 21,500 in Colorado, close to 56,000 in Wisconsin, slightly more than 76,000 votes in North Carolina, 69,000 in Pennsylvania, 56,000 in Ohio, and nearly 86,000 in Michigan. This represents nearly 384,000 votes in the Democratic tallies in just those seven states. (This is based on Democrats receiving three-quarters of non-citizens voting. Richman and Earnest would argue that I might be on the low side.)

While the election on a presidential level and Senate races were not affected; the 2016 North Carolina race between Roy Cooper, the Attorney General who has made opposing voter ID or any steps to reduce non-citizens from voting a central plank and the incumbent governor Pat McCrory most likely was affected, since Cooper beat McCrory by only 12,000 votes.[24]

Our data, backing up what Richman and Earnest reported in their paper, shows that non-citizens do vote, possibly in significant numbers that can be measured in the millions nationwide. We estimate that 2.5 percent of voters in seven key battleground states were non-citizens and that at least one crucial election in 2016, the governor's race in North Carolina could have been affected. Just as Al Franken owns his seat to illegal voters, so could Roy Cooper owe his victory to illegal voters.

The Administrative State

J onathan Turley is a left wing constitutional scholar who teaches law at George Washington University. He wrote a piece in the *Washington Post* in May 2013 on the bureaucratic state that any conservative could have written. It was a searing indictment of the progressive movement as a political ideal. Turley shows how the bureaucratic state is threatening our liberty, which he calls the fourth branch of government.

Turley begins his essay with a brief history and describes how the federal government was small throughout much of our history with only 1,000 non-military workers during Washington's first Administration. Today there are nearly three million federal workers spread across 15 departments, 69 agencies and 383 sub-agencies. Turley notes,

"This exponential growth has led to increasing power and independence for agencies. The shift of authority has been staggering. The fourth branch now has a larger practical impact on the lives of citizens than all the other branches combined." [25]

Turley's point is that this fourth branch has been at the expense of Congress' lawmaking authority. Turley observes; *"In fact, the vast majority of 'laws' governing the United States are not passed by Congress but are issued as regulations, crafted largely by thousands of unnamed, unreachable bureaucrats. One study found that in 2007, Congress enacted 138 public laws, while federal agencies finalized 2,926 rules, including 61 major regulations."* [26]

The point is self-evident; laws are no longer the purview of duly elected legislators but instead are drafted by un-elected bureaucrats. Congress has found itself unable to exert any control over the bureaucratic state and in some cases; many legislators are perfectly willing to allow the bureaucratic state control. Nor, is this all. The judiciary has seen its authority diminish as Congress has given the un-elected fourth branch judicial authority at the expense of the courts. Turley noted, *"These agency proceedings are often mockeries of due process, with one-sided presumptions and procedural rules favoring the agency. And agencies increasingly seem to chafe at being denied their judicial authority. Just ask John E. Brennan. Brennan, a 50-year-old technology consultant, was charged with disorderly conduct and indecent exposure when he stripped at Portland International Airport last year in protest of invasive security measures by the TSA. He was cleared by a federal judge, who ruled his stripping was a form of free speech. The TSA was undeterred. After the ruling, it pulled Brennan into its own agency courts under administrative charges. In the courts, you have due process but under the fourth estate, you are guilty until proven innocent and a citizen is ten times more likely to be tried by a government agency than by the courts!"* [27]

The expansive power of the unelected fourth branch has happened alongside with increase in presidential powers. As Turley observed, *"From the power to determine when to go to war to the power to decide when it's reasonable to vaporize a U.S. citizen in a drone strike. In this new order, information is jealously guarded and transparency has declined sharply."* [28]

On paper, federal agencies report to the White House but in reality, these agencies operate under their own laws, independent of the executive, judicial, or congressional branches. Only one percent of these positions in these agencies are political appointees. Career officials are supposedly insulated from political pressure from civil services rules but as the recent IRS scandal showed; bureaucrats will act in favor of the ruling leftist class. Nor does Turley dismiss this as a product of partisan politics as he observed, *"Today's political divisions are mild compared with those in the early republic, as when President Thomas Jefferson described his predecessor's tenure as 'the reign of the witches.' Rather, today's confrontations reflect the serious imbalance in the system."* [29]

Turley states that common citizens find the bureaucratic state as judge and jury of their guilt but much of this has been hidden from public. The IRS scandal about the harassment of conservative organizations shows the public the abuse of the Fourth Estate as well as the threats the Fourth Estate poses to our liberty. No matter what Congress or the President decides, the Fourth Estate will run the show based on their inclinations! The IRS is a major player on how Obamacare is implemented and the IRS could change Obamacare if they wanted to.

Turley has made a coherent case against the Fourth Estate with which a conservative or libertarian could agree. His indictment should spur efforts to dismantle of bureaucratic state through limiting government and rejecting the Progressive ideology, which has resulted in the un-elected bureaucratic state that is running our lives

Ayn Rand in *Atlas Shrugged* predicted the rise of the bureaucratic state and how it would result in diminution of our liberty. The recent IRS scandal targeting conservative organizations showed the abuse of power and the IRS's threat to our political freedom. The IRS scandal shows how the Fourth Estate is now abusing our freedoms and threatening the very core of society.

Turley concludes, *"We cannot long protect liberty if our leaders continue to act like mere bystanders to the work of government."* [30] He is right, our liberty is at stake—and continually threatened by the political left and the Democratic Party as it is presently constituted.

Class and Race

The left has depended upon identity politics to ensure voter turnout and separate different groups as part of building a winning coalition. They combine race, gender, and class into an effective political force to garner winning majorities. Some conservatives have advocated a strategy of increasing white turnout as a means of winning elections

The vast majority of Trump supporters have legitimate complaints about the problems our country faces. They are not racist or fascist. However, a few within the National Populist movement are moving toward a race identity platform and there are white supremacists who taking advantage of the rise of National Populism to put forward their own supremacist ideas and worse, there are those within the conservative movement that have given them legitimacy.

Breitbart featured an article in the spring of 2016 by Allum Bokhari and Milo Yiannopoulos about the alt-right movement challenging conservatism, which stated, "*There are many things that separate the alternative right from old-school racist skinheads (to whom they are often idiotically compared), but one thing stands out above all else: intelligence. Skinheads, by and large, are low-information, low-IQ thugs driven by the thrill of violence and tribal hatred. The alternative right are [sic] a much smarter group of people — which perhaps suggests why the Left hates them so much. They're dangerously bright…While they can certainly be accused of being overly-eager to bridge the gap between fact and value (the truth of tribal psychology doesn't necessarily mean we should embrace or encourage it), these were the first shoots of a new conservative ideology — one that many were waiting for.*"[31]

Let us be clear about exactly what this new "conservative ideology" entails. Author James Kirchick attended a National Policy Institute forum run by Richard Spencer, a leading promoter of the alt-right agenda. He observed, "*For all their complaints about 'cultural Marxists' and their self-satisfied glee in traducing the prudish dictates of 'political correctness,' identitarians neatly mimic the language of their censorious adversaries on the left. Crude expressions of bigotry are generally frowned upon; today's white supremacists sound much like the campus social-justice warriors they claim to despise, the major difference being their disagreement as to which racial group is most deserving of top-victim status."* Identity politics has replaced past racial slangs but the reality is that they are talking white victimhood to hide white supremacist ideology.

Of many alt-right views of the Constitution including Bill Regnery, a co-founder of the National Policy Institute, Kirchick wrote, *"A mildly enthusiastic Trump voter, he (Bill Regnery) bemoaned the conservative movement for having 'too much involvement with the mechanics of the old America, the Constitution, bromides. Asked to elaborate, Regnery replied that 'the Brits have done pretty well without a constitution and maybe this country would do well without a Constitution.' I was rather surprised by this open disrespect for America's founding document, especially from someone to the right of Genghis Khan. But it turns out that the Constitution is largely unloved, if not outright disdained, among identitarians, who despise it primarily for extolling the virtues of egalitarianism. Writing on the website of Spencer's* Radix *journal, a contributor denigrates the Constitution as a 'primitive article of antiquity' that 'will not solve the problems we face in the 21st century.' Proposing that 'cuckservatives' who speak reverently of the Constitution be denigrated as 'paper worshippers,' 'vellum supremacists,' and 'parchment fetishists,' he argues that the object of their admiration 'has ceased to be a vehicle for progress and has instead devolved into a major obstacle to our future.'"* [32]

Not only are many members of the alt-right adopting much of the Progressives' disdain for the Constitution, they also share the progressive disdain of free market economics and support increased government intervention to obtain their goals. About the need to change capitalism, one alt-right believer wrote, *"The idea behind National Capitalism is to retain the traditional qualities of Capitalism (concentration of the factors of production in the private sector) but without the obsession with deregulation. The goal of national capitalism is to instill in young entrepreneurs a strong and healthy dose of nationalism so that they create businesses that benefit their nations as well as themselves...The working definition of Capitalism has become imperceptibly warped over the decades to refer to a system that prioritizes self-interest at the expense of everything else; nation included. The East Asians don't sub-scribe to this definition of Capitalism and that is why they are beating us."* [33]

Fascism, if it comes to the United States, will come from the left and not the right and it will come in the form of bureaucrats in Brooks Brother's suits. Jonathan Turley and Sen. Ron Johnson (R-Wisconsin), a constitutional legal scholar, summed up this threat to liberty, *"There has been a dramatic shift of authority toward presidential powers and the emergence of what is essentially a fourth branch of government—a vast net-work of federal agencies with expanded legislative and judicial power. While the federal bureaucracy is a hallmark of the modern administrative state, it presents a fundamental change to a system of three coequal branches designed to check and balance each other. The growing authority invested in federal agencies comes from a diminished Congress, which seems to have a dramati-cally reduced ability to actively monitor, let alone influence, agency actions."* [34] While many accuse Trump of being a fascist, as *National Review's* Kevin Williamson and others have pointed out, Sanders is far closer to promoting a Nationalist Socialist vision than Trump.

Most within the National Populism movement who are not associated with the alt-right movement do share the Democratic Socialist distrust of free market economics, limited government and constitutional rule. During the election, we saw that the Democratic Socialism of Bernie Sanders and Donald Trump's National Populism agreeing on quite a lot. Bernie Sanders's Democratic Socialism successfully hijacked the Democratic Party as much of the Democratic Party leadership and politicians are comfortable with Sanders. Steve Bannon, the CEO of *Breitbart* and former chief strategist to President Trump thinks himself a Leninist who wants to burn down the Republican establishment. Free market conservative Steve Moore of the Heritage Foundation told congressional Republicans that the GOP is now Trump's party and it is no longer the party of Reagan. He did so not as crit-icism of Trump but to acknowledge the new reality. [35]

Conservatives, to compete against National Populism and Democratic Socialism, need a new narrative. We need to understand the true nature of the low/zero growth economy and the economic policies that will succeed in a post-industrial revolution world. These policies should break the cycle of zero growth while increasing opportunities to succeed for the middle class.

Lessons of 2016 for 2018 and Beyond

The year 2016 was a watershed year in which both political parties began their evolution toward a new framework with the Republicans facing a more uncertain future while the Democratic Party has moved firmly towards Democratic Socialism, ending whatever moderation may have existed within the party.

The GOP is a party trying to deal with National Populism. Will it be a big government party of right-wing nationalism or a conservative reformist/populist movement that still believes in restricting federal government power? Conservative populists, like National Populists, desire to win the support of blue-collar voters. Other Republicans want to make the GOP the party of Main Street, pursuing a conservative reformist path. The jury is still out which way the Republicans go, while the Democrats have committed their party to their brand of socialism (with crony capitalism for their donors).

This election did not represent any significant realignment. It may have been the last ride of the old Reagan Coalition as the Trump Republicans (formerly Reagan Democrats) came back to the Republican folds, while many economic conservatives and foreign policy hawks came home during the last months of the election, not because of their support or trust of Trump but their fear of Hillary Clinton.

The Democrats depended upon their new emerging majority among Millennials and minorities to prevail in 2016 while writing off blue-collar voters. The Democrats' election strategy was to get enough white voters, including suburban Republican women, while maximizing minority voter turnout.

The Democrats were successful in their goals of gaining support of college-educated Republicans women and as exit polls showed 30 percent of the voters were minorities; a two percent increase over 2012. This led to

Hillary Clinton winning the popular vote. What the Democrats missed was Trump's ability to add blue collar and rural whites to his coalition and, just as important, he gained just enough minority voters winning key battleground states. Moreover, the Democrats' mix of minority voters did not lead to Democratic victories. While Hispanics and Asians increased their vote total but a significant number of blacks, however, stayed home. Enough voted for Trump in battleground states to provide margins of victory. Somewhere between 1 million to 1.5 million blacks either stayed home or voted for Donald Trump, nor can we ignore the 1.3 million leftists who voted for the Green Party candidate, Jill Stein. The number-one voter suppressor of Democratic votes turned out to be Hillary Clinton.

(It should be noted that Hillary Clinton's margin came from one state, California, where she ran more than three million votes ahead of Trump. Take out California and Hillary loses not just the Electoral College but also the popular vote.)

Trump ran ahead of Romney in the popular vote. But two Republicans voted for the Libertarian Gary Johnson for every vote for Johnson by Democrats, according to Fox News exit polls. So when you combine the number of Republicans voting for Gary Johnson and for Evan McMullin, we may be talking a minimum of 1.4 million missing Republicans if not more. (Gary Johnson received nearly 5 million voters and McMullin received nearly three-quarters of a million voters so who knows how many would have voted for Trump if Johnson or McMullin were not on the ballot.) Many of these voters were Never Trumpers who simply would not vote for Hillary Clinton but couldn't bear to vote for Trump either. How many of these voters would have voted for Trump if there were no other viable alternative available. Center of right candidates Gary Johnson, Evan McMullin, and Trump received nearly a million more votes than the leftist candidacy of Clinton and Jill Stein.

In looking at exit polls, we see a shifting of various groups compared to 2012. Trump cleaned up among whites with no college degree with a plus-39 margin, the highest since 1980. But he won White college-educated voters only a margin of four percent. So Trump gained 14 points among non-college educated whites compared to Romney but ran some 10 percent behind Romney among college-educated Republicans. (White college-educated women supported Hillary Clinton.) Overall, Trump had

58 percent of the white voters compared to 59 percent for Romney but he ran ahead slightly among minorities and in key battleground states. He nearly doubled the number of black Republican voters from 2012 and there was a 1 percent drop in black voter turnout compared to 2012. The number of blacks who voted for Donald Trump and the black voters who stayed home could have cost Hillary nearly 1.5 million voters; many of these black voters lived in key battleground states.

In this election, the strength of the Republicans down ballot was shown as in key battleground states as most Republican senatorial candidates ran ahead of Trump. It could be argued that Ron Johnson in Wisconsin, Richard Burr in North Carolina, Pat Toomey in Pennsylvania, Marco Rubio in Florida, Charles Grassley in Pennsylvania, and Rob Portman in Ohio carried Trump in those states. Even losing candidates Kelly Ayotte and Darryl Glenn ran ahead of Trump. (However, Trump did better than Joe Heck in Nevada and Roy Blunt in Missouri.) Republican senatorial candidates won in the key battleground states won by Trump.

Our goal in this book is to review what worked and try to explain why Trump won and how to move forward to 2018 and 2020. Trump dragged the Reagan coalition for one more victory lap but he also has the potential to put a new coalition together or add to his present coalition. The Democrats are now America's socialist party. Over the next four years, they will move harder to the left until they suffer a humiliating election defeat. The Democratic victory in the popular vote reinforces in their mind that this election was a fluke and the eventual emerging Democratic coalition of public sector unions, minorities, single women and the college educated will ultimately lead to victory.

Many issues are going the Republicans' way. Fifty percent of Americans told exit polls that government is doing too many things best left to the private sector and businesses. Only 45 percent wanted government to expand. In 2012, 51 percent of Americans felt government was doing too much and 43 percent wanted government to do more. Our own data supports this view. The big issues favor Republicans and unlike 2012, Americans actually voted for the candidate who came closest in agreeing that government does too much.

CHAPTER TWO

Campaign Successes

Iowa First District

In 2016, Rod Blum faced a major challenge in Democratic candidate Monica Vernon in a district that favored Democrats by a five-point margin. Blum barely won his election in 2014 by two points in a Republican year. His opponent, Monica Vernon, lost the Democratic primary in 2014 but won the 2016 primary by a two-to-one margin in 2016 and had several advantages including she has been a long time political activist in Linn County, the largest county in the First District. She was a former Republican who'd served on the Cedar Rapids city council, first as a Republican in 2007 before switching to the Democrats in 2009.

As a Tea Party conservative, Blum's first act in Congress was not to support John Boehner for Speaker, a move that alienated the National Republican Congressional Committee. But after Paul Ryan became speaker, combined with polls giving Blum a solid shot of winning the district, NRCC decided to support Blum.

Americas PAC enter the race over the last four weeks of the campaign with an ad campaign that featured Blum's record as an independent Iowan fighting to reduce the budget deficit and spending, while Monica Vernon and Hillary Clinton had the same old plan of more government spending and higher taxes.

Blum accomplished two things during the race, the first moving to the center and hugging the coattail of the popular senator Charles Grassley. Many of his ads were identical copies of Grassley ads—working hard for Iowans and solving problems in a bipartisan matter. But Blum also sold himself as a conservative reformer; ready to take on Washington. The Americas PAC ad combined both features of Blum's campaign by talking about Rod Blum being an independent voice for Iowa who worked to pass legislation that saved billions. The Vernon campaign tried to get the ad off the air by threatening one radio station that played it with having its license revoked by the FCC. (This approach failed and the ad continued to run on all of the stations it played on.)

The Loras College Poll polling had Blum at 45 percent and Vernon 38 percent with 16 percent undecided on September 27 before the ad campaign began. Going into the last two weeks, two polls had the Vernon-Blum race even with Blum near 45 percent in both polls. Loras's last poll at the eve of the election had Blum up 47 to 41 with 12 percent undecided.

Most experts said this race would be close. Americas PAC's strategy was to expand Blum's coalition by concentrating on three groups: suburban Republicans, Independents, and Trump Republicans. The ads were on two of the top talk radio WMT 600 (Cedar Rapids) and KXEL 1540 (Waterloo). Both stations covered the entire district and featured popular Iowa talk radio hosts Simon Conway along with Rush Limbaugh and Sean Hannity. These stations targeted Trump Republicans and conservatives. KKRQ 100.7 (Iowa City) and KRNA 94.1 (Cedar Rapids) were classic rock stations that targeted middle age suburban Republicans. We also bought time on KHAK 98.1 (Cedar Rapids), a top country music station that appealed to rural and blue-collar whites

Rod Blum won re-election with 54 percent of the vote. He outperformed Trump in the district, in particular in Linn County, Vernon's backyard, where Hillary Clinton ran nearly 11,000 votes ahead of Trump but Blum ran only 3,000 votes behind Vernon. This allowed him to sprint home with a seven-point margin and polls showed he added 7-9 percentage points over the last two weeks. His ability to reduce the margin to nearly even in Linn County was impressive and he finished 3 points higher than he did in 2014.

Darryl Glenn Colorado Race

D arryl was a heavy underdog, winning an upset win in the Colorado primary. But after the primary, he was far behind Sen. Mike Bennet. In May, he was unknown and this showed up in our polls as Mike Bennet was far ahead. Even after the primary, Glenn was still behind 45 to 39 percent in our poll. Most polls had Glenn far behind, often by double figures. Our polls pointed out serious problems for Glenn, since he was behind among white voters, Independents, minorities, and had only 70 percent support among Republicans.

Many donors shied away from this race since it appeared Bennet would win easily, and while most polls had Glenn far behind, our own poll had this race within six points. Restoration PAC's poll shortly after the primary had Bennet with a one-point lead, but these polls were often ignored even though, in hindsight, they accurately predicted how close the race truly was.

Restoration PAC decided to air a TV ad focusing on Bennet's weakness on national defense and emphasizing Glenn's military veteran experience. Glenn spent 21 years in the Air Force and Air Force Reserves. Americas PAC began a campaign on Hispanic stations to take support from Bennet's base and expanded this into a campaign among white voters, seeking votes from Trump Republicans and suburban Republicans.

With many polls showing double-digit leads going into the final week, our view of the election was that this was a very close race, in lieu of how close Trump was to Clinton in Colorado. Our view proved correct in the final numbers as Bennet won by only 5 percent and Glenn even outperformed Trump, something no polls had foreseen.

Glenn is a case of a candidate losing the election but running a good race when considering the money spent. Glenn was behind among white voters in the summer and in the end, he won white voters. He increased his margin among Republicans significantly, won Independent voters and did better than Mitt Romney in 2012 among Hispanics.

Federal Election Commission filings show Glenn spending $2.3 million in the general election through October 19 and Bennet spending $5.5 million. On October 19, Glenn had $1 million cash-on-hand to Bennet's $3 million. Americas PAC spent $500,000 on radio ads and Restoration PAC added $500,000 on television ads in Colorado. The combined effort supporting Glenn may not have delivered a win, but it made the race close in a way that only Americas PAC expected. Our spending caused Bennet to continue to spend and raise even more money to defend a Senate seat instead of shifting those resources to other states.

Just as Blum and Ron Johnson, Glenn made a charge down the stretch but unlike Blum or Johnson was unable to win. Americas PAC radio program gave Glenn a chance to win and kept him competitive. This race shows that polls can underestimate a candidate's chances and can contribute to having donors shy away from a winnable race, thus denying the candidate the resources he or she will need to ensure victory. If donors understood that the underlying issues favored Glenn and not Bennet, this race could have been a Republican surprise. This campaign did show Super PACs, if running the right campaign based on data and research, can keep an underdog candidate competitive and as we will show; it can propel a candidate to victory, as Ron Johnson did in upsetting Russ Feingold.

Ron Johnson Victory in Wisconsin

S en. Ron Johnson's re-election race for Senate for more than a year was considered futile. He was behind in double digits in most polls, including ours, as 2016 began. Russ Feingold, who Johnson defeated in 2010, was once again running against him with support of the Democratic machine. He looked ready to regain the seat that Ron Johnson took from him.

Our own data showed that even in the summer of 2016, Johnson was running five points behind Feingold among white voters, nearly 10 points behind among Independents, 20 points behind among women, seven points behind among men, and only 70 percent of Republicans supported him. Our data showed that while Feingold was in the lead, Wisconsin voters were concerned about increasing government spending and the rising national debt. Voters also favored economic policies that emphasized growth instead of fighting inequality. These issues favored Ron Johnson.

The Wisconsin primary nearly proved disastrous for Ron Johnson, when many conservatives became Never-Trumpers. Donald Trump attacked Governor Scott Walker often from the left as he often used Democratic talking points on Walker's handling of Wisconsin's economy. Ted Cruz's victory in the Wisconsin primary was as much a repudiation of Trump as showing support for Cruz. For many conservatives, who had witnessed the Democrats protesting Scott Walker in 2011, followed by the recall, the hard 2014 election, and the John Doe investigation, an outsider like Trump mocking what they had gone through to ensure conservative reforms ensured that Trump would receive little support. Ron Johnson had to unite conservatives, moderate Republicans and Trump supporters to re-build the coalition that helped elect Scott Walker three times in four years.

In the summer of 2015, Americas PAC began a radio campaign on both minority radio stations and key stations serving rural and blue-collar whites. The ads on rural and blue-collar stations focused on the economy, while those on radio stations for minorities focused on social issues such as abortions as well as arguing about the Democrat-controlled economy was producing few jobs for them. Our goal was to make Ron Johnson competitive and put him in a position to win.

Our campaign was designed in two parts. The first part emphasized Johnson's issues including his view on controlling budget deficit and increasing job creations. The second part, beginning in the summer of 2016, included increased spending on radio stations for minorities as well as for blue-collar and rural whites, using many of the same stations we used in the first part of our program. Donors liked what we saw and encouraged our efforts.

Based on the Marquette polls, Johnson was consistently behind but at the end of March when the first phrase of the campaign was over, he was within three points of Feingold. As we took a break from advertising, Feingold's lead grew but starting in the summer, we began our fall campaign. As our campaign progressed, the double-digit lead of most pollsters for Feingold started to disappear. Marquette's last poll had Johnson down by one and the Loras College poll had Feingold up by two.

Our campaign was working. Unlike in Colorado, many donors supported us, countering the Democrats who gave millions of dollars to Feingold—money that did not go to Pennsylvania, Missouri or North Carolina where Republican incumbent senators were in trouble. *Our campaign not only gave Ron Johnson a chance to win but it forced Democrats to divert money to a race they thought they won.*

The final results of our campaign were a success. Johnson outperformed Mitt Romney and Donald Trump among minorities as well as Trump. Johnson added 10 points to white voters, 3 points among black voters, 7 points among Hispanic voters, nearly 20 points among Republicans, and 14 points among Independents. This resulted in a 4-point victory over Feingold.

The Ron Johnson campaign may prove to be the model for future Republican campaign combining early campaigning and early polling to see what issues give Republicans an advantage. In addition, targeted use of radio can hit the right voting markets. We tried two programs at the same time; going after the Republican base and Independents as well increasing the minority votes. The program was inexpensive as we averaged 50 dollars per radio ad throughout the whole campaign. This long-term campaign allowed us to dictate the pace of the campaign.

Ron Johnson helped his own cause by campaigning among minorities and aiding minorities, including participating in The Joseph Project, which helps young blacks entering the job market by teaching needed skills—including interviewing skills.

Black Minority Outreach 2016

The 2016 election showed what Americas PAC has known since 2002—minority outreach programs work. This particular election showed the continued the success of minority outreach program in key battleground states.

Despite the success of programs pioneered by the late Richard Nadler, Republicans have been reluctant to spend resources in minority communities because many Republican political operatives thought this was a waste of resources. One candidate in a Midwest state told Illinois Policy Institute CEO John Tillman that there was no reason to put money in minority committee and this politician lost his seat rather handily in the 2016 election.

Since 1964, black voters have given the Democrats 90 percent of their votes. But Republicans' failure to fight for votes in this community has resulted in continued straight party voting among minorities. Democrats routinely used their monopoly in communications to set the tone of the debate by a strategy which could be termed "rape, plunder and pillage" where blacks are told that Republicans would burn their churches, take the vote away from them, and allow police officers to shoot their youth. As Vice-President Biden claimed in 2012, Mitt Romney "is going to let the big banks once again write their own rules, unchain Wall Street. He is going to put y'all back in chains."[36]

During the 2016 elections and working with Americas PAC Tom Donelson as a consultant, The 2016 Committee[37] adopted many of Americas PAC tactics pioneered by the late Richard Nadler and refined by Tom Donelson. The 2016 Committee placed $1,300,000 on radio ads in five battleground states: North Carolina, Ohio, Pennsylvania, Michigan and Ohio. The committee also bought radio ads in two Florida markets—Tallahassee and Jacksonville.

The 2016 committee ran an ad campaign similar to a campaign run by Americas PAC in Louisiana and North Carolina in 2014 that aided in the picking up of two Senate seats by Republicans. Pre-election surveys by major pollsters showed Thom Tillis gaining on Kay Hagan with black voters during the period the ads were running. A final post-election poll conducted by Americas Majority Foundation found that Tillis finished with close to 12 percent of the black votes. The ads may have added 50,000 votes to Tillis. Considering that Tillis won by slightly fewer than 49,000 votes, the ads proved decisive.

In the 2016 election, the committee produced four radio ads that showed how Democratic policies left blacks with inferior education, fewer job opportunities, and more violent neighborhoods. The ads pointed out that black babies were aborted at three times the rate of white babies and asked voters, "Why should I vote for a Party that doesn't want my babies?" School choice and the economy were also subjects of the ad campaign. The ads showed how Democratic policies resulted in black unemployment that was twice that of whites. The ads asked why should Hillary Clinton be able to send her own child to private schools while denying black parents the same opportunity?

Americas Majority Foundation conducted two national polls and also polled seven battleground states including those involved in the 2016 Committee radio programs. In each state, 500-700 black voters were polled.

Donald Trump won all six states where the ads appeared, and Donald Trump became the first Republican to win Wisconsin since 1984 as well as the first to win Michigan and Pennsylvania since 1988. We estimated that Hillary Clinton received 500,000 fewer black votes in 2016 in these states than Barack Obama did in 2012 and 70 percent of the Trump total victory margin in the five states where our statewide ads ran came from just 13 percent of the electorate-African-Americans. In North Carolina and Pennsylvania, black voters who either stayed home or voted for Trump proved to be the Republican margin of victory. Romney averaged 5.2 percent of the black votes in those five states whereas Trump received 9.85 percent, which nearly doubled Romney share.

In 2012, Democrats mobilized African-American voters in record setting numbers. In the states where the ads ran; blacks made up 14.2 percent of the voting population but in 2016, black ballots made up 13 percent of all ballots counted. Trump exceeded the national average in black support by 20 percent in those five states.

States	Percent Vote 2012	Percent Vote 2016	Percent Black participation 2012	Percent Black 2016
Nation	7	8	13	12
Ohio	4	11.5	15	14
North Carolina	4	7	23	19
Pennsylvania	6	10.2	13	10
Michigan	5	12.5	13	15
Wisconsin	7	8	7	7
Total 5 states	5.2 percent	9.84 percent	14.2 percent	13 percent

In Wisconsin, the minority outreach program succeeded in helping Ron Johnson defeat Russ Feingold. Ron Johnson received 50 percent more black votes in his Senate victory than Tommy Thompson when Thompson lost to Tammy Baldwin. Johnson and Thompson had the same number of Hispanic voters. So the increased number of minority voters who supported Ron Johnson helped him win an easy four-point victory over Russ Feingold. (Both Ron Johnson and Tommy Thompson ran ahead of Romney among Hispanic voters and more blacks voted for Johnson in 2016 than voted for Romney in 2012.)

Our pro-Johnson ads targeting minorities were in three phases. First Americas PAC ran ads about how Democrats' plan of high taxes and big spending led to lower incomes for blacks. Then we discussed Ron Johnson's business experience in creating jobs and his charitable work with Project Joseph. Our final ads argued that crime falls when more people were working, and our abortion ads that reminded blacks of the eugenic results of abortion as black babies are aborted three times the rate of white babies. Americas PAC concluded with the question, why should we vote for Russ Feingold when he doesn't even want black parents to have babies? Feingold couldn't answer this question—which is why he lost.

CHAPTER THREE

What Voters Told Us

Do Voters Believe Government Spending Either Helps or Hurts the Economy?

In 2016, Americas Majority Foundation conducted two national polls post-election—one from Voice Broadcasting and the other from Cygnal.

Since 2013 one theme started to appear in polls: Americans feared the intrusion of government in their lives. Americas Majority Foundation associate researcher JD Johannes noted, "For the past forty years as governments at every level have become larger and their debts have grown, the failure of Keynesian economics has become obvious to the public. They have seen government programs expand and public debts become larger while their own personal prospects have remained flat. Fixing the economy and creating jobs is the number one priority for voters. National polls from Pew, Gallup and Rasmussen show the economy has been the top issue for several years. Humans are very good at recognizing patterns, and they see that as the government grows, their opportunities for economic success shrink."

Here are some pertinent findings from recent polls:

A 2013 survey among voters in Illinois found that 55 percent believed increased government spending "hurt their quality of life." This was not just seen among whites but minorities as well. 56 percent of white voters, 49 percent of black voters and 49 percent of Hispanic voters agreed that government spending hurt the economy whereas only 19 percent of white voters, 32 percent of black voters and 14 percent of Hispanic voters felt government spending helped the economy.

In March 2012, the LIBRE Initiative found that 54 percent of Hispanic voters felt that Federal government should reduce spending as a means to aid recovery. Fifty-six percent of Hispanics were concerned about federal government spending and only 36 percent of Hispanic voters believed that their children's economic future would be better than theirs. While many

Hispanics felt that they are reaching the American Dream, they did not have faith in the future. This simply shows many Hispanics are losing faith in the American Dream as lasting beyond the present generation.[38] (Survey of Voter Attitude among Hispanic voters March 2012 Libre Initiative.)

A McLaughlin and Associates poll of young voters in 2013 found that 52 percent felt that government spending hurt the economy, showing that even younger voters understand the risk of government spending.[39]

Gallup asked in 2015 whether the government had too much power and 60 percent of Americans responded yes. Just as three out of every five Americans believe that government spending hurts the economy, three out of every five Americans fear increase government power.[40]

Yet there is a countervailing trend among voters that the government should "do something" to fix the economy.

A poll in October 2013 by Rasmussen found that 52 percent of likely voters are worried the federal government will not do enough to fix the economy, while 37 percent thought the government will do too much, and 11 percent were undecided.[41] This was reversed from 2012 exit polls in which 51 percent of Americans feared government doing too much with only 43 percent saying government was not doing enough.

In an Americas Majority Foundation study on the attitudes of voters in Illinois fall of 2013, we found that 70 percent of respondents agreed with the notion that government spending hurts the economy. In a separate question 70 percent responded that increased government debt "hurts the economy a lot."

In August 2014, Americas Majority Foundation conducted a national poll of Hispanic voters. In the survey, 84 percent of Hispanics rejected Keynesian ideas that government spending helped the economy. Americas Majority Foundation conducted two separate post-election research projects, the first being exit polls among minority voters in four states: New Mexico, Wisconsin, Illinois, and North Carolina. The second survey was a national poll comparing White, Hispanic and black voters' attitude on variety of issues.

In New Mexico, 51 percent of Hispanic voters viewed increase government spending as harmful to the economy, as did 56 percent of Hispanic voters in Wisconsin and 52.5 percent of Illinois Hispanics. In all three states, the majority of Hispanics rejected Keynesian ideas and all three states saw Republican governors elected. In Illinois, Bruce Rauner captured 76 percent of those Hispanics who view increased government spending hurting the economy and he received 38 percent of all Hispanic votes. New Mexico governor Susana Martinez captured 47 percent of Hispanic voters on her way to an easy 14-point triumph and 59 percent of those voters who view government spending with suspicion. Scott Walker beat his Democratic opponent by five points and he took 38 percent of Hispanic voters including 75 percent of those Hispanics who did not support increase government spending supported Walker.

Black voters were more supportive of government spending than Hispanics, as 61 percent of North Carolina blacks supported Keynesian ideas of government spending helping the economy and 53 percent of Wisconsin blacks also supported Keynesian economic policies. Thom Tillis in our exit polls did carry 12 percent of black voters, including 66 percent of those voters who oppose the idea that government spending was good for the economy. (The black view in our post 2014 poll was the only time that any groups in any of our surveys supported the idea of increased government spending helping the economy, but two out of every five blacks still opposed Keynesian economics as method of improving the economy.)

Going into 2016, we argued that Republicans failed to convince voters that they would, get government spending under control and create growth oriented policies that will give voters a fair opportunity to succeed. Voters understand that government can only spend so much and incur so much debt before the private sector gets squeezed. They also know that growing the private sector would give the middle class their opportunity to succeed. The one Republican presidential candidate who understood the voters' frustration was Donald Trump.

Middle class families and minority voters have seen their income drop since 2007. Many minority voters have seen larger drops in their income than whites; giving Republicans opportunities to add minority voters to the conservative coalition, thus damaging Democrats' efforts in future election. We commissioned series of polls among key battleground states over the summer of 2016. Our polls showed that voters continued to oppose additional government spending. In our Wisconsin poll, nearly 70 percent of those surveyed believed that additional government spending hurt the economy, a finding that crossed demographics lines. Nearly three quarters of white and Hispanic voters and nearly 60 percent of black voters viewed increased government spending as harmful. When asked what economic policies should emphasize, Wisconsin voters wanted policies to favor economic growth over dealing with inequality, as 70 percent of the state's voters wanted economic growth, a percentage that was roughly similar for whites, blacks, and Hispanics.

We found that voters in other Midwestern states had concerns similar to those in Wisconsin. In Michigan, 78 percent viewed increased government spending as blocking their economic prosperity, with 65 percent of black voters, 70 percent of Hispanics and 79 percent of white voters agreeing. Seventy-nine percent of Michigan voters supported policies favoring growth over those that dealt with inequality, with 80 percent of white voters, 75 percent of black voters, and 85 percent of Hispanics supporting pro-growth policies.

In Pennsylvania, three out of every four voters in Pennsylvania agreed that increase government spending hurt the economy. Three out of four white and Hispanic voters favored restraint on further government spending along with 58 percent of black voters.

Ohio voters proved to be no different than voters in Wisconsin and Pennsylvania, as 78 percent of Ohio voters opposed raising government spending as a way of helping the economy, with 64 percent of black voters and 80 percent of both Hispanics and white voters agreeing with this statement. In Ohio, 77 percent of voters supported economic policies emphasizing growth over those dealing with inequality, including 70 percent of Hispanic voters, 74 percent of blacks, and 77 percent of whites.

We also conducted polls in North Carolina, Nevada, and Colorado. In North Carolina, 73 percent of voters agreed that increased government spending hurt the economy, including 62 percent of black voters, 72 percent of Hispanic voters, and 79 percent of white voters. Seventy-seven percent of North Carolina voters favored economic growth over inequality, including 74 percent of black voters, 79 percent of white voters, and 78 percent of Hispanics.

In Nevada, three out of every four voters surveyed stated that increase government spending hurts the economy and 62 percent black voters, 72 percent of Hispanic voters, and 78 percent of white voters opposed increase government spending. Seventy-seven percent of Nevada voters also favored economic growth over dealing with inequality and that includes 77 percent of white voters, 71 percent of black voters, and 80 percent of Hispanic voters.

Seventy-two percent of Colorado voters including 59 percent of black voters, 66 percent Hispanic voters, and 73 percent of white voters believed that increase government spending hurt the economy, with 72 percent of Colorado voters favoring economic growth over government policies designed to reduce inequality, including 73 percent of black voters, 76 percent of Hispanics, and 73 percent of white voters.

Early in 2016, Americas Majority Foundation did a national poll to explore how voters viewed issues, including whether they believed that government spending helped or hurt the economy. Our findings in this poll were consistent with those of our battleground state polls. Three out of every four voters rejected the notion that increasing government spending would help the economy, including 72 percent of Hispanic voters, 62 percent of black voters and 78 percent of white voters. Nearly 60 percent of Democrats, 90 percent of Republicans, and 77 percent of Independents believed that increased government spending harms the economy.

In our 2016 national poll, and three out of four voters wanted economic policies favoring economic growth over those dealing with inequality, including 63 percent of Democrats, 89 percent Republicans, and 72 percent of Independents. Even during the primaries, Democrats in exit polls viewed job creation as more important than emphasizing inequality. (Exit polls conducted by the networks during the primaries showed that 40 percent of Democrats wanted policies to grow the economy compared to 26 percent of Democrats preferred policies to deal with inequality),

Our poll is not an outlier but reflects that many Democrats wanted economic growth as a top priority. In our poll, 72 percent of voters agreed when asked if the private sector grows, their opportunity for economic success grows, including 55 percent of Democrats, 88 percent of Republicans, and 77 percent of Independents, as well as 75 percent of whites, 62 percent of Hispanics, and 60 percent of blacks.

We also conducted post–election national polls in 2014 that showed that 61 percent of white voters opposed increased government spending as being good for the economy, along with 53 percent of Hispanic voters. However, only 41 percent of blacks in our poll opposed government spending as being good for the economy. (Our other polls showed that a majority of black voters opposed the idea that increase spending does indeed help the economy.)

In our 2016 post-election polls, one national poll we commissioned from Voice Broadcasting found that only 15.4 percent of voters believed additional government spending would help the economy whereas 67.4 percent believe it will hurt the economy with the rest unsure. Even Democrats questioned additional spending as only 23 percent supported government growth along with 14 percent of Independents and 7 percent of Republicans. Fifty-two percent of Democrats, 83 percent of Republicans, and 68 percent of Independents viewed increasing government spending as hurting the economy. Fifteen percent of whites, 19 percent of blacks, 21 percent of Asians, and 11 percent of Hispanics supported the notion that additional government spending helped the economy, while 69 percent of white voters, 55 percent of blacks, 48 percent of Asians, and 67 percent of Hispanics agreed that increased government spending hurts the economy.

In a second national poll conducted for us by Cygnal, we found that 17 percent of voters agreed that additional government spending would aid the economy whereas 66 percent thought this spending would hurt the economy, with the rest unsure. Supporters of the idea that government spending helped the economy included 8.5 percent of Republicans, 26.5 percent Democrats, and 17 percent Independents, whereas 80 percent of Republicans, 51 percent of Democrats, and 66 percent of Independents oppose the idea that additional government spending will helped the economy with the rest unsure. The pro-government spending side included 17 percent of whites, 21 percent of blacks, 15 percent of Asians, and 20 percent of Hispanics, whereas 67 percent of whites, 56 percent of blacks, 57 percent of Hispanics, and 67 percent of Asians thought increased government spending harmed the economy, with the rest unsure.

We found that regardless of party affiliations and race, voters rejected the need for more government spending as a catalyst for economic growth. We found that voters understood that budget deficit and government debts hurt their opportunity to succeed. Voters also rejected government policies that favored reducing inequality in favor of policies that talked about growing the economy and increasing private sector jobs.

Prevailing Economic Mood from Polls During the 2016 Elections

Throughout the 2016 elections, we saw voters coalescing around four ideas. First, a majority of voters viewed increasing government spending as hurting the economy. Second, the average American views the economy as being rigged, with hard work no longer being rewarded. Third, voters prefer economic policies that increased economic growth over those that dealt with reducing inequality. Fourth, our economic health shapes our ability to influence events abroad. Voters saw that America's place in the world affected their opportunities to succeed, and they understood that a weak economy hampers our ability to project strength abroad. Even Democrats noticed this, as Hillary Clinton ran ads in the primaries that tied economic growth and rising wages to increasing our national security.

Florida voters voiced these concerns in a poll we conducted in January 2016. In our survey, 80 percent of voters agreed that increasing government spending hurts the economy and their opportunity to succeed. This agreed a national poll we conducted in the summer of 2015 that showed that 75 percent of voters viewed increase government spending as hurting the economy, a statement with which 81 percent of women, 79 percent of men, 70 percent of Hispanics, 68 percent of blacks, and 83 percent of whites agreed, as well as 62 percent of Democrats and 60 percent of Hillary Clinton supporters.

Our 2016 spring national poll found 78 percent of white voters, 62 percent of black voters, and 72 percent of Hispanics rejected the idea that increasing government spending helps the economy, a rejection that included 73 percent of men, 77 percent of women, 60 percent of Democrats, 90 percent of Republicans, and 79 percent of Independents.

We found that Florida voters' concerns were similar to our national polls. Seventy-eight percent of Floridian voters wanted policies that emphasized economic growth, and 75 percent of voters also wanted growth oriented policies. Once again, this result was consistent among parties, race and gender. In Florida, 80 percent of men and 77 percent of women preferred job creation over government policies that reduced inequality, a statement with which 74 percent of black voters, 78 percent of Hispanics, and 80 percent of whites agreed, as well as 90 percent of Republicans, 65 percent of Democrats, and 77 percent of Independents.

In our spring 2016 national poll, 75 percent of women and 74 percent of men favored growth policies as well as 63 percent of Democrats, 89 percent of Republicans, and 73 percent of Independents, 73 percent of Hispanics, 74 percent of blacks, and 75 percent of whites.

Our Voice Broadcasting post-2016 election poll found that, 67 percent of voters stated that increase government spending hurt the economy, whereas only 15 percent stated that it helped with the rest undecided. Fifty-two percent of Democrats, 83 percent of Republicans, and 68 percent of Independents stated that increase spending would hurt the economy with the rest undecided, whereas 24 percent of Democrats, 7 percent of Republicans, and 14 percent of Independents stated that increase government spending would aid the economy. Sixty-nine percent of white voters, 55 percent of black voters, 67 percent of Hispanics, and 48 percent of Asians believed that increased spending will hurt the economy, whereas 15 percent of whites, 19 percent of blacks, 11 percent of Hispanics, and 21 percent of Asians said that more government spending was needed to aid the economy with the rest undecided.

In our Cygnal post-election poll, 66 percent of voters stated that increase government spending would hurt the economy, whereas 17 percent viewed government spending as helping the economy with the rest undecided. Eighty percent of Republicans, 51 percent of Democrats, and 66 percent of Independents agreed that increased government spending hurt the economy whereas 8 percent of Republicans, 26 percent of Democrats, and 17 percent of Independents stated it was helpful while the rest were undecided. Sixty-seven percent of whites, 56 percent of blacks, 57 percent of Hispanics, and 66 percent of Asians stated that increased government spending would hurt the economy and 17 percent of whites, 21 percent of blacks, 20 percent of Hispanics, and 15 percent of Asian voters viewed increased spending as helping the economy, while the rest were undecided.

Both polls showed that regardless of party identification and race, a majority of Americans opposed increased government spending as a way to help the economy grow. These numbers have been consistent since 2013, when we began to ask this question.

Finally, we asked voters, "Does the position of the United States as a global leader in diplomacy and military strength affect the economy?"

Among Florida voters, 86 percent of men and 84 percent of women agreed that our place in the world affects the strength of our economy. Agreement on this point crossed partisan, demographic, and gender lines, with 91 percent of Republicans, 76 percent of Democrats, and 84 percent of Independents agreeing, as well as 87 percent of white voters, 79 percent of Hispanics, and 71 percent of black voters.

In our spring 2016 national poll, 85 percent of voters said that America's economy was affected by our place in the world. This statement was agreed to by 85 percent of women, 83 percent of men, 75 percent of Democrats, 93 percent of Republicans, and 86 percent of Independents along with 87 percent of white voters, 77 percent of black voters, and 78 percent of Hispanics.

In our 2016 post-election polls, we continued to find that many voters equate our domestic economic strength with our ability to be a global leader. In our Voice Broadcasting national poll, 78 percent of voters stated that America's place in the world does have an impact on our economy with only 10 percent disagreeing. Eight-four percent of Republicans, 74 percent of Democrats, and 77 percent of Independents agreed with this statement along with 81 percent of white voters, 64 percent of black voters, 71 percent of Hispanic voters, and 63 percent of Asian voters.

In our Cygnal national poll, 63 percent of voters stated that our position as a global leader positively affects our economic status, with 17 percent disagreeing and 11 percent stating that our position has no impact on the economy. Sixty-nine percent of Republicans agreed with this statement, along with 59 percent of Democrats and 61 percent of Independents agreed with the idea that our global position affects our economic position, while 11 percent of Republicans, 20 percent of Democrats, and 18 percent of Independents disagreed, with 9 percent of Republicans, 11 percent of Democrats, and 12 percent of Independents stating it had no impact. Sixty-four percent of white voters, 60 percent of blacks, 58 percent of

Hispanics, and 59 percent of Asians agreed that America's position as a global leader affected our economic status at home, while 13 percent of whites, 15 percent of blacks, 26 percent of Hispanics, and 18 percent of Asians disagreed. 10 percent of whites, 13 percent of blacks, 12 percent of Hispanics, and 14 percent of Asians stating that it had no impact.

Many voters see our position in the world does have an impact on our economic status and while this may be viewed as an esoteric argument, many voters believed our status in the world does sway what happens to their daily life on an economic front.

As Brookings fellow William A. Galston noted in a 2015 column in *The Wall Street Journal*, "Many people who think inequality is an important problem don't believe that Washington's political institution can be trusted to fix it...Negative effects set in only when redistributive measures are piled on top of high levels of existing redistribution." [42] Galston conceded *that increased government spending hurts the economy and the Middle class.*

Nor is this all. Across the board, regardless of gender or race, three out of four Americans preferred a government that stressed economic opportunities and job creation over one that dealt with inequality. Other pollsters have seen this as well. Rasmussen found that voters preferred growth to "fairness" by a 53 percent to 38 percent margin[43] and Democratic pollsters have found similar data. Democratic pollsters the Global Strategy Group concluded in 2014, "More than three quarter of voters (78 percent) believe promoting agenda of economic growth that benefits all Americans should be a very important priority for Congress, and a majority (53 percent) believes such an agenda is extremely important." [44]

John Judis warned his fellow Democrats that pursuing a strategy of using the government to fight inequality could prevent them from being the majority party that can fail at forming a majority, "Unless they can shape their campaign for economic equality so that voters—fearful of big government, worried about new taxes, skeptical about programs they think are intended to aid someone else—are willing to sign on." [45]

In our polls, Democrats favored a government that promoted economic growth over one that fought inequality by a 63 percent to 37 percent margin prior to the 2014 election. In our 2016 Voice Broadcasting national poll, 70 percent of voters favored job creation over reducing inequality, a statement with which with 87 percent of Republicans, 67 percent of Independents, and even 57 percent of Democrats agreed. (Twenty-one percent of the Democrats surveyed thought reducing inequality was more important.). Seventy-one percent of white and black voters supported pro-growth policies, along with 70 percent of Hispanics and 59 percent of Asians.

In our 2016 Cygnal national poll, 67 percent of voters favored job creation whereas 26 percent viewed fighting inequality as more important. Eighty-four percent of Republicans, 64 percent of Independents, and 54 percent of Democrats wanted economic policies to favor job creation, whereas only 9 percent of Republicans, 31 percent of Independents, and 41 percent of Democrats thought reducing inequality a more important function of government. Sixty-seven percent of whites, 68 percent of blacks and Hispanics and 75 percent of Asians supported government policies favoring job creation.

Finally, in our Voice Broadcasting 2016 post-election polls, we asked, "If the private sector grows does the voter opportunity to succeed grow as well?" Sixty-two percent agreed with this statement, whereas 14 percent disagreed and the rest were unsure, with 76 percent of Republicans, 65 percent of Independents, and 48 percent of Democrats agreeing. However, 21 percent of Democrats, 6 percent of Republicans, and 13 percent of Independents disagreed with this statement. Sixty-four percent of white voters, along with 46 percent of blacks, 58 percent of Hispanics, and 62 percent of Asians supported the need for a growing private sector to aid their opportunity to succeed, compared to 12 percent of whites, 22 percent of blacks, 15 percent of Hispanics, and 14 percent of Asians who disagreed.

Our polls show that voters see the need for a vibrant and growing private sector to enhance their own opportunity to earn more income. Trump's victory, in particular his wins in Rust Belt states, was based on voters' belief that he would solve decades of slow growth and reduced opportunities and give voters a new deal to believe in.

Question of Fairness

Many Americans no longer believe the economy is fair and the deck is stacked against them. Voters who blame large corporations, greed and the "one percent" would seem at first to contradict the thesis that conservative economic policies have won and are prevailing. A review of the Pew Research Center's *Trends in American Values 1987-2012* poll finds that 88 percent of Americans "admire people who get rich by working hard" and 63 percent say that hard work is the way to be successful.[46]

Americans admire entrepreneurs, small business owners, family-owned businesses, inventors, creators—but have little respect for managers and traders. It is not the inequality in wealth and income people object to, but the source. The creator, who puts everything on the on the line to start a business, is admired. The manager of a large publicly traded corporation who rises through the ranks without ever having to put any skin in the game is not admired.

The U.S. is still a country where wealth and income earned through hard work and personal risk taking is respected.

Our national survey in 2014 found interesting dynamics. Seventy-one percent of blacks, 79 percent of whites and 66 percent of Hispanics believe that hard work is still rewarded. But when asked if the economic system is rigged against the middle class, 71 percent of blacks, 65 percent of whites, and 61 percent of Hispanics agreed.

In a survey we conducted among Michigan voters in August 2016, two-thirds of white and blacks and 55 percent of Hispanic voters viewed the system rigged against the middle class. But four out of five Michigan voters agreed that to increase economic opportunity and give people a fair chance to succeed, you must grow the private sector. So there is a belief in market economic that is dormant.

Many Americans are seeing that over the past forty years the economy has shifted. As American Enterprise Institute fellow Michael Barone noted in a review of economist Tyler Cowen's book *Average is Over: Powering America Beyond the Age of The Great Stagnation* "wages rose in postwar America because labor was scarce (the 1930s birth dearth) and foreign competition imperceptible. Those conditions ended around 1970. Inequality rose. Perhaps that's the default mode."

Barone, summarizing Cowen, articulates what the public has been experiencing for forty years:

"The big winners in the economy he foresees will be those who can work with and harness machine intelligence and those who can manage and market such people.

"Such 'hyper productive' people, about 15 percent of the population, will be wealthier than ever before. Also doing well will be those providing them personal services.

"For jobs lower down on the ladder, there will be a premium on conscientiousness. That's good for women and bad for men, who are more likely to do things their own way.

"Middle-level jobs, Cowen says, are on the way out. He argues that many of those laid off after the financial crisis were 'zero marginal product' workers. They weren't producing anything of value and employers won't replace them." [47]

Middle class and family income has declined, and they haven't even reached the pre-recession numbers of 2007. Median incomes are lower now than the median income when the recession officially ended in 2009, and are lower now than in 2007.

In today's economy, more people live on welfare and are below the poverty line, resulting in an increased need for food stamps. During the Obama years, incomes went down and the number of food stamp recipients went up.

Climate Change and Energy Development

Another issue that will benefit Republicans is talking about job creation and energy development. The fear of climate change has paralyzed national debate on energy, but the good news is that many voters despite being told for years that climate change is the fault of man, are not sold on the idea.

In 2011, Americas Majority Foundation did two surveys that included questions on climate change. The vast majority of voters either believe that climate change is naturally induced or caused by human activity combined with natural events, instead of being exclusively caused by human activity.

In a study on contrasting investors with non-investors, 50 percent of minorities with investments believed that climate change was caused by natural events combined with human activity while another 32 percent said the climate changed solely by natural events. Even minorities without investments, 40 percent said climate change was due to a combination of natural events and human activity while another 31 percent believed it was due to natural events alone. Eighty-two percent of minority investors and 86 percent of white investors believed that climate change was due to either natural events or a combination of natural events and human activity while 71 percent of black non-investors and 81 percent of white non-investors supported the idea that climate change was due to either natural events or a combination of natural events and human activity. This showed that the vast majority of voters including minorities, accept the position of most climate realists or skeptics. Sixty-six percent agreed that climate change has happened in the past so we don't need to alter our lifestyle.

In our national poll of Hispanic voters conducted in August 2014, 75 percent of Hispanics believed that climate change is either due to a combination of natural events and human involvement or simply natural events alone, a view supported by 68 percent of New Mexico Hispanics, nearly 68 percent of Wisconsin Hispanics, and 62 percent of Illinois Hispanics.

We found in our post 2016 national polls that voters continue to reject the climate alarmist view that human activity is the primary reason for climate change. Our Voice Broadcasting poll found that 24 percent stated human activity was the primary reason for climate change, but 43 percent stated it was natural causes combined with human activity and another 25 percent said it natural causes were the primary reason. This showed that voters accepted the scientific arguments of climate skeptics *since skeptics have argued that climate change was caused by natural events but many skeptics also view that human activity could play a role combined with natural events.*

Ten percent of Republicans, 25 percent of Independents, and 35 percent of Democrats accept the alarmist arguments that climate change is exclusively due to human activity, whereas 55 percent of Democrats, 79 percent of Republicans, and 67 percent of Independents agreed that climate change is caused either by a combination of human activity and natural events or natural events alone. Twenty-four percent of white voters, 21 percent of blacks, 18 percent of Hispanics, and 35 percent of Asians thought that climate change was only caused by human activity while 78 percent of whites, 62 percent of blacks, 66 percent of Hispanics, and 56 percent of Asians said that climate change was due to either natural causes or a combination of natural causes and human activity.

In our Cygnal poll, 29 percent of voters believed that human activity exclusively caused climate change whereas 21 percent of voters believed that natural events caused climate change and 46 percent thought climate change was due to a combination of human activities and natural events. Forty-three percent of Democrats thought human activity was the only reason for climate change while 54 percent accepted the skeptic arguments. Republicans supported the skeptic arguments by a margin of 81 percent to 14 percent, while the support for climate skepticism among Independents was 67 percent to 25 percent. Our polls show that when voters are given all of the scientific arguments from both the skeptics and alarmists, they overwhelmingly reject climate alarmists. This finding is consistent among thousands of voters we have polled since 2011.

We asked in past polls, including our post 2014 poll, whether we should first deal with climate change or emphasize job creation. In our post-2014 poll, 73 percent of whites, 77 percent of blacks, and 74 percent of Hispanic voters said that dealing with job creation was more important than dealing with climate change.

In our 2016 post-election polls, we found a division. We asked voters whether energy policy should exclusively emphasize expansive energy development and economic growth or consider climate change as part of any energy policy. In the Voice Broadcasting poll, 48 percent stated economic growth takes precedence whereas 36 percent says climate change must be taken in consideration, with the rest unsure. In our second poll, 37 percent stated economic growth should be the primary goal and 44 percent viewed that climate change should take precedence. In both polls, Republicans favored economic growth whereas Democrats favored energy policies taking climate change in consideration. The difference was in Independents. In the Voice Broadcasting poll, they favored energy expansion, while in the Cygnal showed Independents believing that climate change must be considered in energy policy. In the Voice Broadcasting poll, whites, blacks, Hispanics, and Asians all favored economic growth but in the second Cygnal poll, whites, blacks, Hispanics, and Asians said that climate change should be considered in decisions about energy policy.

The good news in these surveys is that these opinions have occurred in spite of the media's unanimously saying that humanity is responsible for climate change. We asked in 2011, "Have you heard of "Climategate?" 67 to 75 percent of black, white, and Hispanic voters said no. Climategate was the scandal in a tranche of thousands of leaked emails showed that many climate alarmists admitted that much of their data was methodologically flawed. Our poll showed that between 67 and 75 percent of black, white, and Hispanic voters said they had never heard of Climategate. This question told us that many Americans are not aware of the major debate within the scientific community about the degree to which climate change is occurring.

It is a miracle that many voters have rejected the climate alarmists' theories and offer a common-sense approach—that natural events are part of climate change. Our two post-election polls from 2016 show that most Americans believe that climate change is partially caused by human activity and is partially natural and that many Americans want more energy developed.

Voters respond to growth oriented arguments. The best case that Republicans and conservatives can make is that extensive energy development means cheaper energy and cheaper energy, combined with business-friendly tax policies, gives American companies a reason to stay in the United States.

Voters on Gold Backing the Dollar

During the 2016 election, we asked voters for the first time about monetary policy. We asked if the dollar should be based on a weight of gold. Much of the world was on a gold standard before World War II, and even after the war, the world was on a dollar standard and the dollar was connected to gold until Richard Nixon removed that connection in 1971.

In **Colorado**, in May 2016, 35 percent of Colorado voters agreed that the dollar should be backed by the weight of gold, with 28 percent disagreeing and the rest having no opinion. Eight weeks later, 41 percent agreed that the dollar should be based on the weight of gold whereas 29 percent disagreed. Every major demographic group saw an increase for their support for the gold-based dollar but there were significant differences between political parties. In May, 45 percent of Republicans agreed that the dollar should be based on the weight of gold with only 17 percent disagreeing, and eight weeks later 52 percent of Republicans supported tying gold and the dollar with only 18 percent opposed. Twenty-two percent of Democrats in May 2016 and 26 percent of Democrats eight weeks later supported the concept of a dollar based on gold, contrasted to 40 percent of Democrats disagreeing in May and 43 percent disagreeing eight weeks later. (Note we ran two separate polls in Colorado and Nevada as part of testing ads.)

In **Nevada**, a plurality of voters supported the concept that the dollar should be based on the weight of gold. In May, 41.6 percent of voters supported a gold-weighted dollar followed by 40.6 percent of voters eight weeks later, while only 26.5 percent of voters opposed this in May and 28 percent eight weeks later. Blacks were least likely in Nevada to be supportive, with 28.4 percent of blacks in May supportive followed by 35.7 percent eight weeks later. In May, 28 percent of blacks opposed having a dollar supported by gold, followed by 33.8 percent eight weeks later. While black support for the gold standard increased, there was an even split between support and opposition for the gold standard. Nevadan Hispanics were the strongest backers among ethnic groups, as 47.7 percent of Hispanics supported the gold standard in May and 50 percent eight weeks later. White support nearly mirrored the overall voter support, as 42.2 percent in May supported the gold standard vs. 40.4 percent in July, while only 26.4 percent opposed the Gold Standard in May and 28 percent in July. Republicans in Nevada were more likely to support the gold standard than Democrats, as 51.4 percent in May and 48.8 percent of Republicans in July supported the gold standard, compared to 26.2 percent of Democrats in May and 28.7 percent Democrats in July.

The closet margin was in **Wisconsin** where 29.4 percent supported the gold standard while 28.5 percent were opposed. Blacks opposed the gold standard by a 28.5 percent to 27.7 percent margin, whereas 30.7 percent of white voters supported the gold standard while 27.4 percent were opposed. Hispanics supported the gold standard by a 37.3 percent to 36.4 percent margin. Wisconsin Republicans and Independents were more supportive of having a dollar backed by a weight of gold, whereas Democrats opposed the idea. Thirty-eight percent of Republicans supported the gold standard while 21 percent opposed it, and 32 percent of Independents favored the gold standard compared to 31 percent opposing, but only 23 percent of Democrats supported a dollar backed by gold whereas 32 percent opposed.

Ohio voters agreed that the dollar should be supported by a weight of gold, by a 39 percent to 24 percent margin, with Republicans supporting the need to tie the dollar to gold by a 47.5 percent to 16 percent margin, with Independents favoring tying the dollar to gold by a 42 percent to 24 percent margin where Democrats opposed the idea by 35.5 percent to 24 percent. Blacks approved tying the dollar to gold by a 31 percent to 29 percent margin, whereas both whites supported the gold standard by a 39 percent to 24 percent margin. Hispanics were more supportive, favoring the gold standard by 43 percent to 16.5 percent opposed.

In our Voice Broadcasting 2016 post-election national poll, 37 percent voters supported the dollar to be supported by a weight of gold and 28 percent said no, with the rest unsure. 46 percent of Republicans and 40 percent of Independents supported the gold standard, which was supported by only 25 percent of Democrats. Opponents of the gold standard included 35 percent of Democratic voters, 21 percent of Republicans, and 27 percent of Independents. Supporters of the gold standard included 37 percent of whites, 32 percent of blacks, 33 percent of Hispanics, and 35 percent of Asians who wanted dollar to be backed by a weight of gold whereas 28 percent of whites, 29 percent of blacks and Hispanics, and 26 percent of Asians said no.

In the Cygnal national poll, 41 percent of voters favored a weight of gold backing the dollar and 30 percent opposed it. The gold standard was backed by 47 percent Republicans, 41 percent of Independents, and 35 percent of Democrats, whereas 24 percent of Republicans, 36 percent of Democrats, and 36 percent of Independents opposed the idea with the rest unsure. Forty-one percent of whites, 44 percent of blacks, 34 percent of Hispanics, and 19 percent of Asians favored a weight of gold backing our dollars whereas 31 percent of whites, 25 percent of blacks, 42 percent of Hispanics, and 53 percent of Asians opposed this.

Monetary policy does affect trade policies as President Trump has made currency manipulation part of his attack on China, but it could easily be argued that the Fed's quantitative easing is also currency manipulation and the advantage of having currencies backed by gold would make it more difficult to manipulate the currency. The gold standard does have its disadvantages, since it imposes discipline upon government spending and many nations have chosen to escape the standard rather than discipline their spending.

We are not recommending one particular monetary policy over the other, but stable money is a necessity for long-term economic prosperity, and central bankers are often encouraged to inflate the currency to allow governments to fund massive spending program and to aid in increasing exports. Nor does long-term inflation help the economy as many businesses can't plan ahead if they are not certain what their investments will be truly worth.

There hasn't been a debate on monetary policy in the U.S. since 1896, when Democratic presidential candidate William Jennings Bryan wowed his party's convention by saying that "you shall not crucify mankind on a cross of gold."[48] Certainly no modern-day politician, with the exception of Ron Paul, has brought up the importance of the gold standard.

Judy Shelton noted in *The Wall Street Journal*, "Nevertheless, *Mr. Trump's emphasis on currency manipulation brings into focus the short-comings of our present international monetary system—volatility, persistent imbalances, currency mismatches—which testify to its dysfunction. Indeed, today's hodgepodge of exchange-rate mechanisms is routinely described as a "non-system. No wonder so many workers employed by U.S. companies that manufacture products requiring substantial capital investment—automobiles and tractors, computer and electronic equipment—have become disenchanted with the supposed long-term benefits of free trade. It is one thing to lose sales to a foreign competitor whose product delivers the best quality for the money; it's another to lose sales as a consequence of an unforeseen exchange-rate slide that distorts the comparative prices of competing goods…To brand trade skeptics as sore losers is to malign them unfairly. To resent being victimized by currency movements is not the same as being opposed to free trade, nor does it signal an eagerness to engage in protectionist retaliation. It's simply an honest response to incongruity: We need to reconcile global monetary arrangements with global trade aspirations…As former Federal Reserve Chairman Paul Volcker has observed: "Trade flows are affected more by ten minutes of movement in the currency markets than by ten years of (even successful) negotiations."* [49] Shelton's point is that monetary manipulation affects trade negatively and if central bankers can't maintain monetary stability, they are putting the benefit of free trade at risk.

Voters are willing to explore re-instating the gold standard, but many voters have no opinion on this issue, and no more than 41 percent of voters overall view a dollar backed by a weight of gold as a good thing. So unlike trade issues where both voters and presidential candidates have strong opinions, most voters and politicians do not have a strong belief in what constitute good monetary policy, even though a government that inflates their money is hurting their ability to succeed.

Voters' View of Free Trade

In exit polls in the 2016 primaries, when asked if trade helps or hurts American job creation, the voters answered trade hurts job creation. Republican primary voters, by a 55.8 percent to 32.9 percent margin, said that trade hurt job creation with the remainder saying that trade had no impact on job creation. Democrats were more supportive of trade, but even 45 percent of Democratic primary voters stated trade hurt job creation compared to only 38 percent that believed it helped job creation. Primary voters rejected liberalized trade in those states that this question was asked.

The rise of Donald Trump on the Republican side and the Bernie Sanders challenge forced Hillary Clinton to change her view on trade. This is a strong indication that voters are rejecting the concept of liberalized trade between nations. Fifty percent of Republicans who viewed trade as having a negative impact on jobs supported Donald Trump, more than his overall vote total of 41 percent during the competitive stage of the primary season. Thirty-four percent of voters who viewed trade as positive backed Trump.

Among Democrats, Hillary Clinton received 57 percent of those who rejected trade as a source of job creation and close to 50 percent of those voters who believe trade supports job creation. These high numbers reflected Hillary Clinton's own evolution from supporting trade (including the Trans-Pacific Partnership) to encouraging trade restrictions.

Other polls have supported this view that Americas have turned against trade as a mechanism for job creation and increased opportunities. Bloomberg Politics earlier this year after the Iowa Caucus conducted a national poll in which nearly two-thirds of Americans favored more restriction on imported goods and this cut across politics, race, gender, education, and income [50]. Pollster Ann Selzer, who oversaw the survey, declared that on trade there is unity of opinion. This was supported by a recent

Rasmussen poll in which respondents believed our government didn't do enough to support American business against foreign competitors.[51]

In the Bloomberg Politics poll, one question asked if a community be better off with an American company that employed 1,000 workers or a Chinese-owned company employing 2,000 workers. Sixty-eight percent of the respondents preferred the American company that hired half of the numbers of workers. Eighty-two percent of respondents stated they would pay "slightly more" for goods made by an American company. When asked about NAFTA, 44 percent of the respondents viewed NAFTA as hurting the economy, with 29 percent saying that has been positive and the rest having no opinion. Democrats were more supportive of NAFTA, with 38 percent saying it was good for America and 36 percent saying it was bad for America, whereas 53 percent of Republicans and 46 percent of Independents said that NAFTA was bad for America. (Ironically, Republicans in the House helped pass NAFTA as the majority of Democrats voted against the treaty. Without Newt Gingrich, President Bill Clinton would not have been able to pass NAFTA.)[52]

A Pew Research Center survey during the 2016 primaries showed that Trump supporters viewed the proposed Trans Pacific Partnership treaty (TPP) as hurting America by a 59 percent-17 percent margin and all trade treaties as bad for America by a 68 percent-26 percent margin, contrasted to the general population who viewed free trade negatively, but by only a 47 percent-45 percent margin, and favored the proposed TPP agreement as a good thing by a margin of 39 percent-37 percent. Democrats are more supportive of all trade by a 59 percent-32 percent and the TPP by a 55 percent-24 percent margin, while Republicans agreed that "free trade is a bad thing" by a 53 percent-38 percent margin.[53]

Both Donald Trump and Bernie Sanders used protectionism as a means to enhance their campaign and in the case of Trump, eliminating bad trade deals as part of an overall strategy of increasing jobs opportunities for America. Sanders's success led to Hillary Clinton's abandonment of free trade, an important achievement of her husband's administration that spurred job creation. She accepted Sanders's argument that a liberalized trading system is responsible for lower wages and a declining middle class.

Gallup however bucked this trend with their own poll, done in the spring of 2016. In the poll, 58 percent of respondents agreed that trade increased opportunity for economic growth through U.S. exports whereas slightly more than a third viewed foreign export as a threat to the economy. [54] When Gallup asked the question again in February 2017, they found 72 percent of those surveyed saw foreign trade as a key to economic growth. This was the highest support for foreign trade ever recorded in a Gallup Poll. [55]

In 1992, 48 percent of those surveyed believed that trade was good for job creation as opposed to 44 percent viewing trade as a hindrance. Three years later, voters supporting trade went up to 53 percent vs. 38 percent oppose. What happened in those three years? In 1992, Ross Perot made trade and his opposition to NAFTA as one of his cornerstone issues and throughout the 1992 elections, you had one voice opposing increased liberalized trade. Over the next three years, the Clinton Administration working with the Republicans in Congress led by Newt Gingrich passing NAFTA as the leadership of both parties defended free trade. [56]

A *Wall Street Journal*/NBC news poll conducted in July 2016 mirrored the Gallup poll, as 55 percent of respondents viewed trade as good for America, including 60 percent of Democrats, 54 percent of Independents, and 51 percent of Republicans. [57] So like Gallup and unlike Bloomberg Politics, this poll shows that the issue of trade is not yet settled and that there is room for a candidate to move up the ladder who promotes free trade as a mechanism for increased job creation and opportunity for the middle class to move up the ladder.

Gallup editor in chief Frank Newport observed, *"Over the life span of asking this question, the imports/negative viewpoint prevailed in 1992 (during a bad economy) and even before (and during) the recession of the mid-2000s. The opportunity/positive viewpoint was on top in 1994 and in the early 2000s, and has soared back on top in the past several years. We've had four consecutive years now in which the majority of U.S. adults have come down on the positive side of the foreign trade equation as measured by this question... But other questions measure Americans' attitudes in different ways. A set of questions on trade was released recently by Bloomberg with the headline: "Free-Trade Opposition Unites Political Parties in Bloomberg Poll.".....The wording of the central question about trade in that poll was: "Turning now to trade, generally speaking, do you think U.S. trade policy should have more restrictions on imported foreign goods to protect American jobs, or have fewer restrictions to enable American consumers to have the most choices and the lowest prices?" The results showed 65 percent agreeing with the first option, 22 percent agreeing with the second and the rest not sure. Several observations about this question: The question focused just on "imported foreign goods" and didn't mention or deal with exports, the other half of the foreign trade equation. Free trade agreements work both ways, and removing restrictions on imports is usually coupled with removing restrictions on exports. This question focuses on the bad —or more negative—side, and in isolation, it might not be surprising that the public is more likely to agree with the "more restrictions" option...The question includes the highly potent concept of "jobs." If there is one thing I've learned about public opinion and the economy, it is that Americans react positively to the idea of creating more jobs. It's the No. 1 thing Americans talk about when we ask them how to improve the economy, and a number of proposals made by the presidential candidates that include the idea of creating more jobs test extremely well. Thus, when this question includes the option to "protect American jobs," it is not surprising that it receives a majority response."*[58]

Newport's point is that if you present trade in bad light, you will get a negative answer toward trade, and if you present it in a positive light, you will get positive responses.

Americas Majority Foundation conducted six surveys of four battleground states over the summer of 2016: Nevada, Colorado, Wisconsin, and North Carolina involving 14,000 voters between May through the first of July 2016. (Two polls were conducted in Colorado and Nevada eight weeks apart.) Our results were similar to *Wall Street Journal*/NBC News and Gallup and ran counter to what exit polls were showing and Bloomberg's results. We modeled the question similar to what voters were asked in exit polls but with one difference. Voters in exit polls were asked if trade helped or hurt job creation whereas we asked if *free trade* was good or bad for jobs. Did the word "free" in front of trade make consumers more favorable towards trade?

In North Carolina, 51.6 percent of voters stated that free trade enhanced job creation, whereas 35.5 percent viewed it as an obstacle to trade with the rest saying free trade had no impact on jobs. Blacks, Hispanics, and whites all agreed that free trade was good but in North Carolina, Democrats were more likely than either independent and Republicans to view trade as good for Americans. Nearly 55 percent of Democrats viewed trade as good compared to 50 percent of Republicans and 47 percent of Independents.

In Wisconsin, 50.7 percent of voters viewed trade as positively supporting job creation compared to 34.5 percent opposing free trade. More than half of whites and Hispanics viewed trade as good for job creation and 49 percent of blacks viewed trade positively. Only 36 percent of whites, 32 percent of blacks, and 33 percent of Hispanics viewed trade as hurting economic growth.

In Nevada, voters' views changed very little in our two polls. In May 2016, 54 percent of voters in May viewed as trade as good for job creation and 55 percent eight weeks later viewed trade positively. White voters showed very little change, with 55 percent in May supporting trade compared to 56 percent eight weeks later. Black voters had a slight drop in support for trade from 49 percent to 48 percent. Only Hispanics showed a significant drop from support for trade. With 59 percent in May approving of trade compared to 54 percent eight weeks later. In all three groups, the majority or plurality viewed trade as good for job creation.

Our Colorado survey saw voters support for free trade increase by a wide margin with 57 percent in May supporting trade and 59 percent supporting it eight weeks later. In May, 59 percent of whites viewed trade as positive and 61 percent agreed with the pro-trade view eight weeks later. Both black and Hispanic voters saw their support for trade increase from May to July, with nearly 52 percent of blacks and 42 percent of Hispanics viewed trade as positive in May and 58 percent of blacks and 53 percent of Hispanics approved of trade eight weeks later. In our Colorado surveys, the only group that viewed trade negatively was Hispanics in our first Colorado survey, with 47 percent of Hispanics viewing free trade in May 2016 as an obstacle to jobs growth.

Among Republicans in Colorado, support for free trade over the eight-week period held firm at 61 percent but Democrats' support for free trade rose from 53 percent to 60 percent in our two polls, while Independents' support for trade rose from 51 percent to 58 percent.

Ohio voters supported free trade by a 50 percent to 38 percent margin with Republicans supporting trade by 56 percent to 35 percent, Independents by 47 percent to 39 percent, and Democrats by 44 percent to 41 percent. White voters supported free trade by 50.5 percent to 39 percent, blacks by 50 percent to 37 percent, and Hispanics by 51 percent to 37 percent. Exit polls during the primaries showed Ohio Republicans rejecting trade as being good for jobs by a 55 percent to 33 percent and Democrats primary voters viewed trade equally harmful by a 53 percent to 28 percent margin.

In election exit polls, just as they did in exit polls in the primaries, voters viewed trade as hindering job creation, even though their support was less than in the primaries. Our 2016 post-election Voice Broadcasting poll found that 44 percent of voters viewed free trade as helping economic growth and 28 percent saying it hurt job creation and 7 percent saying trade had no impact. This support was consistent among both parties and all races. In the Cygnal poll, 42 percent of voters viewed free trade as helpful to job creation, while 35 percent said that trade hurt job creation with 9 percent had no impact. Just like the first national poll, voters' agreement that free trade creates jobs was consistent among both parties and all races.

Why the differences? Between our primary polls and our exit polls? It's possible that the issue of trade is not settled and that our polls are outliers just as Gallup's is an outlier. It could also be that our summer polls of battleground states were done after the presidential primaries, so many voters did not think carefully on their views on trade. But the biggest reason may simply be the campaign itself. Throughout both primaries, the defense of free trade was non-existent. Except for Marco Rubio, who would defend trade when asked in debates, no Republican discussed the benefit of trade as part of the general campaign whereas Donald J. Trump viewed trade barriers and "negotiating better trade deals" as part of his overall strategy to increase jobs for the middle class. The Democrats had two candidates that supported the protectionist agenda with no pushback. In a one-sided debate, the side that makes their case will win against the side that stays on the sideline.

Gun Rights
Gun Rights and Minority Voters

L iberal advocacy and interest groups have created the impression that Hispanics tend to favor more laws regulating and restricting firearms. Latino Decisions, a polling and research firm that works for Democrat campaigns and private sectors corporations, conducted a poll in February 2013 showing that Hispanics support gun control laws. The respondents heavily favored background checks (84 percent) but there was less support for banning "semi-automatic and assault weapons" (44 percent) and limiting "the number of bullets and ammunition that guns can hold" (62 percent).[59]

The Latino Decisions poll showed support for generically worded gun control proposals.

But there is a gap between supporting generic descriptions of proposed laws and supporting actual laws. The most obvious gap is in the gap between supporting a generic proposed law and thinking it will actually be effective. As indicated by the results of a 2013 Reason-Rupe poll, 52 percent of Democrats think new gun control laws will "_not_ be effective in preventing criminals from obtaining guns." [60]

Polling by Gallup on crime and firearms ownership finds that 60 percent of gun owners say they own a weapon for "personal safety/protection." The same survey shows that respondents feel crime is increasing.[61]

In a poll conducted among Hispanic voters in 2014, we found that 62 percent of English-speaking Hispanic registered voters in Illinois strongly agree that "people should be able to own a gun to protect their family and home" but that this statement had far less support among Spanish speakers.

A solid majority (55 percent) of Spanish-speaking respondents agreed that people should be able to own a gun to protect their home, but only 46 percent agree there is a constitutional right to own a gun. But a note of caution—acknowledging a constitutional right is not the same as absolute support for it. For the respondents who "strongly agree" many of them could easily be strongly agreeing with the fact that there is a Second Amendment.

Owning a gun to protect family and home clearly resonates as a point of agreement among Hispanic voters and will be a stronger point of advocacy than an abstract constitutional right.

As noted above, the polling by Latino Decisions shows support among Hispanics for new gun control laws, but our polling confirms the gap noted by the Reason-Rupe poll. Hispanic respondents, whether they primarily speak English or Spanish, were not convinced new restrictions would make their neighborhoods safer.

Identifying gun restrictions with Democrats created an interesting result. English speakers gave slightly higher marks to Democratic restrictions, while Spanish speakers moved in the opposite direction. We found that Hispanic voters are not convinced new gun control laws will make their neighborhoods safer and could be open to alternative policies to improve public safety.

This final point has been verified by other studies we conducted. In a national poll of Hispanic voters conducted in August 2014, only 15 percent of Hispanic voters viewed the need for more gun laws while 41 percent stated we should enforce existing laws and 38 percent believed that the community should be more active in defending their neighborhood.

Post-election polls in 2014 among minorities showed similar results. Twenty-five percent of North Carolina blacks and 19 percent of Wisconsin blacks supported the need for new laws, while 35 percent of North Carolina blacks and 34 percent of Wisconsin blacks favored enforcing existing laws. Finally, 39 percent of North Carolina blacks and 46 percent of Wisconsin blacks supported parents and community taking more control of their safety.

Our polls found that 22 percent of Hispanics in New Mexico, Illinois, and Wisconsin combined supported the need for new gun laws but 36 percent believed that existing laws needed to be reinforced, while 42 percent supported the need for parents and the community taking control of their personal safety.

In a national poll following the 2014 election, we saw agreement among Hispanics, blacks, and whites on gun rights issues as well. Twenty percent of white voters, 21 percent of black voters, and 18 percent of Hispanic voters saw the need for new laws, but 40 percent of white voters, 31 percent of black voters, and 37 percent of Hispanic voters said that we needed to enforce existing laws. Thirty-nine percent of white voters, 47 percent of black voters, and 44 percent of Hispanics supported the need for parents and communities to protect their neighborhood.

Women and Gun Rights

Do unmarried, female registered voters believe there is a difference between a constitutional right to own a gun, a right to protect your home and family, and a right to protect your home and family with a gun?

A poll of unmarried, female, registered voters in Colorado that we conducted found that 92 percent said that people have a right to protect their home and family. When asked if people have a right to protect their home and family with a gun 71 percent agreed. This is strong support for framing the firearms debate in favor of rights to protect home and family rather than abstract constitutional rights. The study found that comfort with a gun in the home was a decisive predictor of support for gun rights.

In 2008 Gallup asked if the Second Amendment "guarantees the rights of Americans to own guns" and 63 percent of non-gun owners said there was a right. Unmarried women are far less likely to own a gun than men. The Gallup poll breaks the question down by gun owners and non-owners. Not surprisingly 91 percent of gun owners say the Second Amendment guarantees a right to own a gun.[62]

Gun Rights and Community Safety

Gun rights advocates would gain further ground by emphasizing the right to self-defense. This is one issue where Republicans and conservatives have the upper hands. While minorities may support gun laws, they prefer to own guns for their self-defense. Milwaukee County, Wisconsin, Sheriff David Clarke showed that an African-American defending gun rights *can* survive a Democratic primary in his 2014 primary victory.

We found similar results in our 2016 post-election polls. In many battleground states, voters prefer a combination of community efforts to defend their neighborhoods or enforcing existing laws. In Wisconsin, only 23 percent of voters favored additional laws to protect their rights to guns compared to 37 percent recommending enforcing existing laws and 29 percent saying that parents and neighbors should take control of their community. In Nevada, only 22 percent of voters wanted new laws while 70 percent preferred either enforcing existing laws or having communities responsible for their own protection. In Colorado, only 22 percent of voters favored adding new laws while 68 percent preferred either enforcing existing laws or having communities responsible for their self-defense. In our post-election surveys of voters in Michigan, Pennsylvania, North Carolina, and Ohio, we found that only 17 to 25 percent of voters surveyed saying that additional laws were needed for community protection.

Voters in the national Voice Broadcasting 2016 post-election poll preferred enforcing existing laws over adding additional anti-crime laws, as only 24 percent voters wanted new laws and 40 percent wanted existing laws enforced, while 30 percent favored giving neighbors and parents the right to defend their communities. Eight percent of Republicans and 21 percent of Independents in this Voice Broadcasting poll favored new laws, whereas 54 percent of Republicans and 40 percent of Independents wanted enforcing existing gun laws. Among Democrats, 39 percent wanted new laws while only 27 percent favored enforcing existing laws. Supporters of the right to have communities protect themselves included 33 percent of Republicans, 27 percent of Democrats, and 32 percent of Independents. Twenty-four percent of white voters, 25 percent of blacks, 20 percent of Hispanics, and 36 percent of Asians favored new laws to protect gun use while 42 percent of white voters, 30 percent of black voters, 38 percent of Hispanic voters, and 22 percent of Asian voters supported enforcing existing laws. Twenty-nine percent of white voters, 37 percent of black voters, 36 percent of Hispanic voters, and 30 percent of Asian voters supported the concept of self-defense.

In our Cygnal national poll, only 20 percent of voters wanted additional gun laws whereas 30 percent favored enforcing existing laws. We added a question on parents' involvement with their children would help make neighborhoods safer and 29 percent agreed with this statement, while an additional 10 percent wanted communities to be more effective in their own self-defense. Seven percent of Republicans, 20 percent of Independents, and 32 percent of Democrats wanted new laws whereas 37 percent of Republicans, 31 percent of Independents, and 21 percent of Democrats stated they wanted existing laws enforced. Twenty-one percent of whites, 19 percent of blacks, 16 percent of Hispanics, and 14 percent of Asians wanted new laws whereas 31 percent of whites, 24 percent of blacks, 29 percent of Hispanics, and 35 percent of Asians want existing laws enforced. An additional 10 percent of whites, 13 percent of blacks, 5 percent of Hispanics, and 13 percent of Asians wanted neighborhoods to take more initiative to defend themselves against criminals. Twenty-eight percent of whites, 31 percent of blacks, 37 percent of Hispanics, and 27 percent of Asians wanted parents to be more involved with their children to increase safety of their neighborhood.

The polling evidence suggests that most voters prefer to have existing gun laws enforced rather than passing new laws. We found in many polls that not only do voters want existing laws enforced, but they also want their communities to have more power to defend themselves. Republicans and conservatives need to stress the ability of a community to defend themselves and enforce laws on the books, since many voters will agree with those views. Even Democrats have recognized that voters prefer gun rights to more gun control, which is why they were hoped to stack the courts with enough judges to overturn both *McDonald* and *Heller* to enforce their own vision of gun restriction through the Courts, since they have failed to get voters to support their gun-control agenda.

Abortion

Over the past two years, we found that many minorities are social conservatives and definitely pro-life.

Following the 2012 election, a survey we conducted with Illinois Hispanics found that 56 percent viewed themselves as pro-life. The following June, Hispanics by a plurality of 37 percent to 36 percent still declared themselves pro-life and white voters viewed themselves as pro-life by 46 percent to 45 percent.

Americas Majority Foundation after the 2014 election surveyed 5200 Hispanics, nearly 4,000 black voters and 1,200 white voters and our data showed that many Americans can be classified as pro-life and do not object to restriction on abortions, with the only debate being where to place restrictions.

In a summer 2014 survey, 51 percent of Hispanics viewed themselves as pro-life with 44 percent saying they consider themselves pro-choice. Our 2014 post-election poll found that 15 percent of white voters, 12 percent of Hispanics, and 19 percent of blacks believe that abortion should be allowed in all circumstances, compared to 20 percent of whites, 17 percent of blacks, and 22 percent of Hispanics who believe that abortion should be prohibited in all cases. Thirty-seven percent of white voters, 40 percent of black voters, and 43 percent of Hispanics believe that abortion should be allowed only if a woman's life is in danger or if she is impregnated due to rape or incest. Twenty-seven percent of white voters, 23 percent of black voters, and 21 percent of Hispanic voters are willing to allow abortions in the first trimester but are open to restricting abortion in the second and third trimesters unless the mother's life is in danger.

Our survey showed that, 57 percent of white voters, 57 percent of black voters, and 65 percent of Hispanic voters either favor complete prohibition of abortion or prohibit abortion with minimal exceptions. Our findings could be interpreted as saying that the majority of Americans favor restrictions of abortion, but will argue about where to draw the line.

In 2014, the Democratic "war on women" fizzled as most voters including many women viewed economic issues as their number one concern. Exit polls did not mention abortion in their top four issues and in the 2014 election, the economy was the primary concern of Hispanics and black voters. However our data does show that being pro-life helps attract minority voters.

Dealing with pro-life ads, Tom Donelson and Adam Schaefer concluded about their ad test among nearly 1,800 Hispanics, "Many libertarians in the conservative coalition argue that in order for the GOP to win elections, it needs to tack left on social issues. But among Hispanic swing voters, we discovered that the truth is closer to the opposite: Socially conservative appeals can make people more likely to trust the GOP on *economic* issues."[63]

In our 2016 post-election polls, we saw some differences between the Voice Broadcasting and Cygnal polls, due to two ways to look at abortion. Pro-life positions can be identified as no exceptions to abortions or restrictions of abortions in the first trimester while allowing for exceptions for the life of the mother or in cases of rape and incest. Pro-choice advocates may allow restriction in abortions in the second or third trimesters or simply have no restrictions on abortions. The second way to look at abortions is to ask if voters favor any restrictions starting in the second or third trimester. Throughout the 2016 elections, the questions of restricting abortions in the second or third trimester became an issue as Trump in the final debate made the case that Clinton's position on abortion forbade any serious restrictions in the final trimester.

In the Voice Broadcasting national poll, 55.7 percent of voters favored the pro-life position, including restricting abortions in the first trimester or complete prohibition of abortion, whereas 36.7 percent favored unlimited abortions or not imposing restrictions until the second trimester. But 71 percent of voters believe that abortions should be restricted, including restrictions in the second or third trimester. So at least seven out of ten voters in this poll reject the notion of unlimited abortion rights. Seventy-two percent of Republicans accept the pro-life positions, compared to 39 percent of Democrats. By contrast, 21 percent of Republicans and 51 percent of Democrats accept the pro-choice position. In this survey, 57 percent of Independents favored the pro-life position with 37 percent being pro-choice. Eighty-five percent of Republicans, 56 percent of Democrats, and 77 percent of Independents favored restrictions on abortions. Fifty-six percent of white voters, 48 percent of black voters, 57 percent of Hispanics, and 39 percent of Asians support the pro-life positions whereas 38 percent of white voters, 38 percent of black voters, 30 percent of Hispanics, and 35 percent of Asians support pro-choice positions. However, 71 percent of white voters, 62 percent of black voters, 71 percent of Hispanics, and 51 percent of Asians accept restrictions on abortion.

In our Cygnal poll, 46.4 percent of voters favored the pro-life positions and 46.2 percent favor the pro-choice positions, with 65 percent favoring restrictions including pro-choice advocates who accept restrictions on abortions in the second and third trimesters. Sixty-three percent of Republicans, 31 percent of Democrats, and 44 percent of Independents favor the pro-life positions whereas 30 percent of Republicans, 42 percent Democrats, and 49 percent of Independents favored pro-choice positions, while 80 percent of Republicans, 51 percent of Democrats, and 64 percent of Independents favor restrictions. Forty-seven percent of white voters, 45 percent of black voters, 38.5 percent of Hispanic voters, and 33.5 percent of Asian voter's support what is consider the pro-life position, whereas 45 percent of white voters, 46.5 percent of black voters, 57 percent of Hispanic voters, and 67 percent of Asian voters favor the pro-choice position. However, 66 percent of white voters, 62 percent of black voters, 64 percent of Hispanics, and 48 percent of Asians favor restrictions on abortions.

The Cygnal poll shows that while there is a division between pro-life and pro-choice voters, many Americans support pro-life positions, including restrictions on abortion. The debate is over whether these restrictions begin in the first trimester or within the final weeks of pregnancy. Americans don't accept that abortions should be unrestricted but the question is where those lines need to be drawn. Considering that more evangelical voters supported Donald Trump than blacks and Hispanics combined supported Hillary Clinton, abandoning the rights of the unborn does not necessarily gain Republicans votes. Many minorities do support abortion restrictions, so there are no political gains to be had forgoing a pro-life position *and may even interfere with Republicans efforts to increase minority support.*

Immigration

Since 2004, when George W. Bush got the support of slightly more than two of every five Hispanic voters, Republicans have lost ground among Hispanic voters over the next election cycle, and Hispanics played a central role in the 2016 election in key battleground states, particularly Nevada and Colorado.

The Pew Research Center, in a survey of Hispanic voters before the 2014 election, noted that 54 percent of Hispanic voters could support a candidate who disagreed with them on immigration but one third of Hispanics would vote against a candidate who disagreed with them on this issue.[64] To what extent will this become an issue for Hispanics and how will immigration affect the in future elections?

We noticed a change in Hispanics' attitude on immigration in our August 2014 Hispanic survey. After a massive exodus of children from Central America, many Americans became aware that the Obama administration seemed not to be concerned about border security. This and the threats from the Ebola virus may have been a game changer; many Americans viewed border security as crucial for further immigration reform.

When asked certain options in our August 2014 poll of Hispanics, 20 percent of Hispanics supported border security before any further immigration reform, whereas 16 percent of Hispanics favored allowing those who were here illegally to stay provided they had a job, but not be given a way to obtain citizenship. By contrast, 49 percent wanted a path of citizenship for illegal immigrants who were here, with the remainder either not knowing or saying they supported other unidentified ideas for dealing with illegal immigrants

In a 2014 post-election poll conducted among Hispanics in Wisconsin, New Mexico, and Illinois, 27 percent of Hispanics favored no immigration until border security was addressed whereas nearly 19 percent of Hispanics favored to allow illegals to stay but not offer them a path to citizenship. Thirty-six percent believe that illegal immigrants should be given a path to citizenship and 18 percent favored other options not identified in our poll.

Exit polls we did for black voters in Wisconsin and North Carolina in our 2014 post-election polls showed that, 20 percent of blacks favored restricting immigration until border security was addressed whereas 19 percent favored allowing illegals to stay in the country but not offered a path to citizenship while 36 percent believed illegal immigrants should be offered a path to citizenship while 24 percent believed in other options.

In our national poll following the 2014 election, 27 percent of black voters and 26 percent of Hispanic voters did not support further immigration reforms until the border is secured, while 17 percent of black voters and 23 percent of Hispanic voters supported allowing illegal to stay in the country without no path to citizenship while 33 percent of black voters and 35 percent of Hispanics supported illegal immigrants staying in the country and being offered a path of citizenship, while other options were supported by 22 percent of black voters and 15 percent of Hispanic voters. Forty-five percent of white voters supported border security before any discussion of any immigration reform, while nearly 14 percent supported allowing illegal immigrants to stay without being given a path to citizenship, while nearly 23 percent said that illegal immigrants should be given a path to citizenship. The rest supported other options.

There are two ways to view our findings. Less than half of Hispanics support a path to citizenship, but 55 to 65 percent of those surveyed in the three polls we conducted in 2014 supported options allowing illegals to stay and two thirds of those favoring legal status for illegals supported a path to citizenship. (Fifty percent of black voters in our national poll supported options that allow the immigrants to stay in the country, whereas only 38 percent of white voters preferred this option.)

In our 2014 national poll, 65 percent of white voters and 56 percent of black voters believed that additional immigration took away jobs whereas 54 percent of Hispanic voters believe that immigration aided job creation. Hispanics were more willing to support options to allowing illegals to stay in the country but only 35 percent to 49 percent of Hispanics supported a path to citizenship for illegals outright.

If the Pew Research Center findings are right, many Hispanics are willing to listen to Republicans on other issues even if they disagree with them on immigration. In 2016, Democrats used immigration as a wedge issue to get Hispanics out to vote. While Hispanics increased their turnout by 10 percent, more Hispanics voted for Trump than voted for Romney in 2012.

Hispanics are not a monolithic group as they have as varied a demographic as white voters and, as we have already seen, many Hispanics do have views similar to other white voters. Further confusion can be seen in our 2014 summer survey when Hispanics were asked, should the children who entered the country last summer be allowed to stay, 80 percent said yes, but when asked, "Would you want those children moved to your neighborhood?" nearly 60 percent said no! While it can be argued that Hispanics support ways to allow illegals to stay here, this support is not as overwhelming as one supposes.

In our two separate 2016 national polls, the Voice Broadcasting poll produced results similar to data produced in 2014, while the Cygnal poll had a different result as far as what to do about providing a path to citizenship for illegal aliens. But both polls showed similarity as to what future immigration levels should look like.

In the Voice Broadcasting poll, 39 percent of the voters opposed any further immigration reforms until the border were secured, while 11 percent stated they would allow immigrants legal status provided they had a job but offer a path to citizenship while 37 percent stated they wanted illegal immigrants to have a path to citizenship.

Fifty-eight percent of Republicans and 40 percent of Independents favor no further immigration until the border were secured while only 19 percent of Democrats wanted to wait for the border to be secured before allowing more immigration. Twenty percent of Democrats, 10 percent of Republicans, and 12 percent of Independents favored allowing illegals to stay without giving them a path to citizenship, providing the illegals had a job. Fifty-five percent of Democrats and 35 percent of Independents favored allowing illegals a path to citizenship, whereas only 19 percent of Republicans favored this citizenship path. Forty percent of whites, 26 percent of blacks, 27 percent of Hispanics, and 34 percent of Asians favored no further immigration reform until the border was secured, while

11 percent of whites, 17 percent of blacks, 13 percent of Hispanics, and 16 percent of Asians favored providing legal status for illegals provided they had a job, but not offer them a path to citizenship. Thirty-six percent of whites, 41 percent of blacks, 47 percent of Hispanics, and 39 percent of Asians favored providing illegal immigrants with a path to citizenship.

In the Cygnal poll, 34 percent of voters wanted no further immigration until the border was secured, while 47 percent favored a path to citizenship for illegal immigrants and 10 percent favored allowing a legal status for illegals but no path to citizenship. The division in these two polls shows that there is a divided America on this issue, as one poll had border security given priority over any path to citizenship and the other viewed a path to citizenship for illegal immigrants as more important than border security.

Fifty-one percent of Republicans, 18 percent of Democrats, and 33 percent of Independents in the Cygnal poll wanted tightened border security before proceeding with any further immigration, while 64 percent of Democrats and 47 percent of Independents favored a path to citizenship for illegals with only 30 percent of Republicans supporting a path to citizenship. Ten percent of Republicans, 9 percent of Democrats, and 11 percent of Independents favored allowing legal status for aliens based on employment status, but not offering a path to citizenship. Thirty-six percent of whites, 21 percent of blacks, 21 percent of Hispanics, and 28 percent of Asians wanted border security implemented before any further immigration reform but 45 percent of whites, 55 percent of blacks, 60 percent of Hispanics, and 55 percent of Asians favored a path to citizenship for illegal immigrants. Twelve percent of whites, 12 percent of blacks, 14 percent of Hispanics, and 12 percent of Asians favored allowing legal status but no path citizenship.

Americas Majority has numerous polls in which the support for legal status was lower than the Cygnal poll. But the polls suggest that most minorities favor legal status for illegal immigrants, not all polls showed that a *majority of minorities believe in a path to citizenship for illegals*. Whites as a group favored legal status for illegal immigrants but less than half favor a path to citizenship for illegals. Throughout the Republican primary, a majority of Republicans favor legal status for illegals, and in exit polls, 70 percent of voters favored legal status, but in neither case did pollsters ask what "legal status" meant. In our poll we did ask that question and got a more definite answer of what voters wanted when we distinguish between whether an immigrant should be granted a path to citizenship or simply allowed to stay with no path to citizenship.

Another question rarely asked is the level of future immigration. While many polls may ask whether immigration is good for America or ask about legal status, rarely do we get an insight on whether voters actually want immigration levels to stay the same, be reduced or increase. Here we see there is a consensus being formed.

In the Voice Broadcasting poll, 49 percent of voters favored reduced levels of immigration, while only 26 percent favored either keeping the level the same or increased, with the rest unsure. In the Cygnal poll, 51 percent of voters wanted a reduction in immigration levels while only 33 percent wanted immigration levels increased or staying the same. In the Voice Broadcasting poll, 68 percent of Republicans and 50 percent of Independents favored reduced immigration levels while 12 percent of Republicans and 26 percent of Independents wanted levels to be increased or remain the same. Thirty-one percent of Democrats wanted reduced immigration, while 40 percent wanted more immigration or having immigration levels stay the same. In the Cygnal poll, 64 percent of Republicans and 47 percent of Independents wanted reduced levels while only 19 percent of Republicans and 36 percent of Independents wanted to see increased immigrations or immigrations stay the same. Thirty-nine percent of Democrats favored reduced levels while 46 percent wanted to see immigration levels either stay the same or increased.

The Voice Broadcasting poll showed that 51 percent of white voters, 38 percent of black voters, 40 percent of Hispanic voters, and 42 percent of Asian voters wanted to see immigration levels reduced, while 25 percent of white voters, 29 percent of black voters, 33 percent of Hispanic voters, and 41 percent of Asian voters wanted to see immigration levels increase or stay the same. In the Cygnal poll, 53 percent of white voters, 41 percent of black voters, 46 percent of Hispanic voters, and 50 percent of Asian voters wanted to see immigration reduced while 31 percent of white voters, 40 percent of black voters, 45 percent of Hispanic voters, and 36 percent of Asian voters favored increased immigration levels or levels remaining the same.

While Democrats favored increased immigration, significant numbers of Democrats would love to see immigration levels reduced, and a majority of Republicans and a plurality of Independents favored lower levels of immigration. Nearly half of Hispanics in our 2016 polls favored reducing immigration levels. This is a change from 2014, when a majority of Hispanics viewed immigration as positively benefitting for the economy while other groups rising immigration as harming the economy. It's arguable that more Hispanics favor lower immigration levels than oppose supporting increasing levels, and even many Hispanics doubt if increased immigration levels will actually stimulate the overall economy.

This points to a possible compromise on immigration reform, with a significant number of Americans favoring border security as a perquisite for further reform. While Americans favor legal status and a path to citizenship for illegal immigrants, they also want future immigration levels to be reduced to allow for assimilation and don't view increased immigration as helping them personally. So any reforms that combine providing a way for citizenship for illegal immigrants, enhanced border security, and reductions in future immigration have a chance to pass. (One of the great secrets of the election was that the Trump reform when completed would have resulted in nearly the same number of illegals allowed legal status as other plans.) The difference was that Trump reforms don't happen until the border is secure and those illegals with criminal records are deported. Republicans are moving toward a future immigration plan that reduces future immigration levels—a point on which most Americans, including minorities, agree.

Republican Gap with Women Voters Begins with Minority Voters

The Republican Party does not have a problem attracting women voters. It has a problem attracting *minority voters*, both male and female. The aggregate of 9,000 plus interviews with registered voters in 2012 Gallup's tracking poll shows that 50 percent of white women favor Romney with only 41 percent preferring Obama.[65] In final 2012 exit polls, this margin increased to 12 percent as Romney carried 56 percent of white women to Obama's 44 percent.[66] Married poll respondents favor Romney over Obama 54 percent-39 percent.[67] If you are looking at a married, white woman, you were likely looking at a Romney voter.

Obama's electoral advantage in women was with unmarried, minority women. Conservative strategists looking to mitigate Obama's lead among women should focus on minority women who are struggling under the failure of Democratic economic policies.

In 2012, single females went for Obama by a two to one margin[68] and when one reviews the data, it is not hard to understand why. Most single females make less than their married counterpart and many minority single females also have children and live in poverty or close to the poverty line.

Thirty-five percent of black families headed by single parents live in poverty compared to 7 percent of married black families and 38 percent of Hispanic single female head of household hold live in poverty compared to 12 percent of married Hispanic couples. Living in a single parent home increases the chances of children living in poverty and receiving government assistance, thus more likely to support big government programs and income transfers.[69] But those programs have done nothing to help women and children rise out of poverty.

Marriage is a significant factor in poverty and as Heritage Foundation senior fellow Robert Rector noted, "Marriage remains America's strongest anti-poverty weapon. As husbands disappear from the home, poverty, and welfare dependence will increase. Children and parents will suffer as a result." Family structure plays a factor in combating poverty and the evidence shows decline in family formation plays a role in the number of minorities in poverty.

In 1930, only 6.3 percent of children were born out of wedlock but today that number has risen to 40 percent. Thirty-six percent of single parents live in poverty compared to 6.3 percent of married couples. Only one out of four two-parent families with children are poor when contrasted to nearly 71 percent of families headed by a single parent, showing that family formation is a significant factor in poverty. While many blame teen pregnancy for the increase in single parents, three out of five unwed children are born to women aged 20–29. The least educated women are more likely to have children out of wedlock. Sixty-seven percent of women without a high school degree have children out of marriage whereas mothers with college degrees or higher have 8.3 percent chance of having children out of wedlock.

Education is a factor in whether a woman will have a child out of wedlock but regardless of education, married women are less likely to live in poverty than single parents. Only 15 percent of women who are married and without a high school diploma live in poverty, whereas 47 percent of single female head of household dropouts live in poverty. Thirty-one percent of single female head of households with a high school diploma live in poverty compared to only 5 percent of married families, and 24 percent of single female head of households with a

ollege degree live in poverty while only 3.2 percent married women with a college degree live in poverty. Nearly 9 percent of single women with a bachelor's degree or higher live in poverty compared to 1.5 percent of married families where couples have a bachelor's degree or higher. Something has obviously gone horribly wrong with family formation; the hardest hits are minority women and children.

"The gag rule about marriage is nothing new," Rector writes in his Heritage Foundation report. *"At the beginning of the War on Poverty, a young Daniel Patrick Moynihan (later Ambassador to the United Nations and Senator from New York), serving in the Administration of President Lyndon Johnson, wrote a seminal report on the negative effects of declining marriage*

among blacks. The Left exploded, excoriating Moynihan and insisting that the erosion of marriage was either unimportant or benign. Four decades later, Moynihan's predictions have been vindicated. The erosion of marriage has spread to whites and Hispanics with devastating results. But the taboo on discussing the link between poverty and the disappearance of husbands remains as firm as it was four decades ago." [70]

Marriage is the key to eliminating poverty because it causes husbands to earn more for the family. As Manhattan Institute fellow Kay S. Hymowitz pointed out, "Marriage itself, it seems, encourages male productivity. One study by Donna Ginther and Madeline Zavodny examined men who'd had "shotgun" marriages and thus probably hadn't been planning to tie the knot. The shotgun husbands nevertheless earned more than their single peers did."[71]

As long as couples decline to marry, the ability of policymakers to institute policies to raise minority families out of poverty may have limits. What is clear from the past 50 years is that the path away from poverty is not more government assistance, but jobs, economic growth and encouraging two-parent families.

The question that remains is how much is being a single female voting Democratic dependent upon being a minority. The conservative campaign strategy of benign neglect toward minority voters is the source of the "women gap" for Republican candidates. Romney after all led Obama in 2012 among white women and Trump continued this in 2016. Minority women are a significant factor in the Democratic lead among women in general and single women in particular.

In 2016, Hillary Clinton carried women voters 54 percent to 41 percent while Trump carried male voters 52 percent to 41 percent [72] but looking at the data more closely, we found that minority women not only voted overwhelmingly for Hillary, they also voted more heavily for Hillary than minority males.

While Trump ran behind Romney among white college educated women, he still carried white women by 52 percent to 43 percent while carrying white males by 62 percent to 31 percent. Thirteen percent of black males voted for Trump and 33 percent of Hispanic males voted for Trump compared to only 4 percent of black females and 25 percent of Hispanic women. Trump won college educated white males with 53 percent, as well as 62 percent of non-college white educated women and 71 percent of non-college educated white males. Only college educated white women voted for Hillary Clinton. (A majority of white college educated women did vote for Romney, so Republicans might want to hope this is a one-election blip.) Trump did not perform as well with college-educated whites but he did sweep non-college educated white women and males.[73]

As the data shows, the Republican gender gap with females begin with minority voters and it should be noted that black women make up 58 percent of overall black voters compared to 54 percent of Hispanics voters being women and 52 percent of white voters are female. Black women make up a greater number of the overall black voters and this adds to the gap of women voters between Republicans and Democrats.

To close the gap, Republican strategists need to recognize the "gender gap" is not with women in general, but minority women who have been hardest hit by failed Democratic policies

Youth Voters and Minority Voters Are Connected!

With the exception of bailed out bankers and recipients of green technology loan guarantees, every economic sector and demographic group were hit hard by the Great Recession. The demographic group suffering the most is young people aged 18 to 29, with young African-Americans and Hispanics the hardest hit. They directly felt the brunt of the Obama administration's failed economic policies.

The Republican gains among young voters in 2010 showed there is an opportunity to develop a new generation of voters who will embrace the GOP's job-creating economic policies. Understanding this potential new cohort of voters and how to reach them requires a close look at their underlying demographics because young voters are rapidly becoming minority voters.

*"The surge in the minority vote we saw in 2008 **was** the surge in the youth vote,"* Sean Trende writes in his book *The Lost Majority.*[74]

Trende observed that Obama's lead among all voters, including the18 to 24 age cohort, was less pronounced once non-white voters were taken out of the calculation. *"These groups swung toward Obama largely because these segments of the electorate became much more heavily minority in 2008, as the country continued to "brown "demographically and as Obama turned out minority voters in droves...It does suggest GOP does not have a minority problem and youth problem. It is the same problem."*[75] The younger a voter is, the more likely the voter is an ethnic or racial minority. Only 57 percent of Americans between 18 and 29 are white. Attracting young voters and minority voters should be seen as a unified effort for national Republican campaigns and in states like California, Texas, Florida, and Illinois.

The Democrats continue to count on an upsurge in minority voters as well as youth voters. In 2008, Obama garnered 66 percent of the youth vote, which is the first time that either party gathered above 60 percent among young voters 18 to 29. When minorities are taken out of the mix of young voters, Obama's margin was not much different that the general election results of 54 percent to 46 percent. Among 18–29-year-old voters in 2008, Hispanics voted for Obama 76-19 and African-Americans voted 96-4. Hispanic youth voted more for Obama than other Hispanic age groups. Hispanic voters over the age of 30 gave Obama 62 percent, less than Obama's 67 percent overall vote total among Hispanics. Hispanic youth voters added five percentage points toward Obama's total percentage among Hispanic voters. Youth voters provided the difference in Obama's winning North Carolina and Indiana, two traditional red states, in 2008.

Who were the youth voters in 2008? The youth voters were 18 percent African-Americans compared to 13 percent for the overall population, 14 percent Hispanics compared to 8 percent in the overall population, whereas only 62 percent whites make up those voters 18 to 29, compared to 74 percent of the overall voting population. Minority voters helped to push the overall minority voting total to record setting numbers. Over the last three election cycles, 2008, 2012, and 2016, minority voters have made up a larger youth voting pool than in the past. In 2000, whites made up 74 percent of voters 18 to 29, and by the 2008 election cycle, whites made up only 62 percent of this age cohort.[76]

In 2012, Romney carried young white voters by 51 percent to 44 percent, but just as McCain did in 2008, Romney lost the minority vote by wide margins. Hispanic youth voters went for Obama 74 percent to 23 percent and many of those young people who voted in 2008 for Obama, continued their support in 2012. Hispanics and black youth voters increased their support of Obama from 2008 and added to the overall increase of minority voters from 2008 for Obama.

Ruy Teixeira and John Halpin, in their 2011 study for the Center for American Progress, "The Path to 270,"[77] predicted that minority voters would make an even larger share of voters in 2012 than they did in 2008, and while these Democratic strategists conceded that Obama would not match the 80 percent of minority voters he received in 2008, they forecasted that Obama would receive 75 percent of minority voters. They anticipated those extra minority voters would lead Obama to victory if other segments of the Democratic coalition showed their support. They proved to be correct.

In 2008, Obama and the Democrats were more effective in contacting young voters by a two to one margin than the McCain campaign and this led to increase voter turnout among young voters. In 2008, minority young voters contributed significantly to both increase vote totals to Obama and the added turnout among minority voters in general. The Obama campaign found that a minority get out the vote campaign led to an increase in young voters.

On a campaign-by-campaign basis, with a focus on winning *this year,* the return on investment of specific efforts to reach out to young and minority voters is low for most U.S. House campaigns. For Senate campaigns, presidential campaigns and the long-term competitiveness of the Republican Party, attracting young minority voters is a smart move. Young voters who have been borne the brunt of Obama's failed economic policies should have been primed to support the job creating economic policies of Republicans.

In 2000 and 2004, youth voters nearly split between being registered Republicans and Democrats, but in 2008 young voters affiliated with the Democratic Party by a nearly 2 to 1 margin. Republicans cut the deficit to 13 percent in the 2010 midterm election when they lost the youth vote by only a 55 percent to 42 percent margin. [78]

In 2016, Hillary Clinton captured 56 percent of the 18–29-year-old voters compared to 36 percent to Trump so the GOP made inroads compared to 2008 and 2012. Just as in 2012, minority voters paved the way for Hillary to win the youth votes. Trump carried young white voters 47 percent to 43 percent and while white voters made up 70 percent of the total voters, they made up only 63 percent of youth voters. Hillary carried 85 percent of Black youth voters compared to 9 percent for Trump and Hispanics youth voters went for Hillary by a margin of 68 percent to 26 percent. If there is any hope, Trump did slightly better among black youth voters than older black voters. [79]

The conservative movement can't cede African-Americans and Hispanic voters. Young minorities need exposure to conservative views and understand how these ideas will yield real, tangible results in jobs and personal financial success.

Americas Majority Foundation's chief economic researcher Brad Furnish, observes, "Unfortunately, establishment Republicans have been traumatized by the demonization they have suffered at Democrat hands. They want to take the easy way out by hiding from confrontation instead of seeking it out. The time is ripe for this outreach. A black President has done absolutely nothing to improve the lives of blacks. A Republican Presidential candidate is openly advocating policies - such as vouchers - that blacks have long favored to remedy one of the most conspicuous failures of 20th-century liberalism." (Furnish wrote this for me as part of an interview. Furnish, like me, worked with Richard Nadler from the formation of Americas PAC and also wrote for Nadler's magazine KC Jones. He, like me, was at the ground zero of Americas PAC.)

The outreach Furnish advocates is an advertising campaign on urban and Top 40 radio, and digital platforms that lays bare Democrats' failure to create jobs and contrast the Democrats failed policies with conservative ideas.

Republicans have a message of hope for young minorities looking to climb the economic ladder. Minority unemployment is higher than among whites and many minority communities are seeing depression levels of unemployment. Cities like Detroit collapsed under decades of Democratic control.

The increase of minorities among young voters, in particular Hispanics, should convince Republican strategists of the need to increase their voting base beyond the rural-suburban white base to include more minorities. African-Americans and Hispanics do have many conservative ideas and a high percentage of minorities should be natural allies of the conservative movement. Republicans have followed a political strategy of benign neglect where they have ignored many minority communities, but now that strategy can no longer be followed. As minorities become a larger part of the population, Republicans and conservatives need to start making inroads and 2018 may be the election to begin the process of winning the future and setting the stage for an expanded conservative majority.

CHAPTER FOUR

Toward A New Foreign Policy

The Rise of the Anglosphere

James C. Bennett and Michael J. Lotus in their book *America 3.0* [80] see the end of the bureaucratic state, or what they call "the end of America 2.0," and return to a smaller and more decentralized "America 3.0." Bennett and Lotus begin with a brief history of how we got to where we are at present, as we moved from being an agricultural America 1.0 to an industrial America 2.0. What Bennett and Lotus present is not just a roadmap toward a new America over the next quarter century domestically, but a new foreign policy based on the one alliance that will prove dependable for the next century, an alliance of the Anglosphere nations: United States, Great Britain, Canada, Australia and New Zealand.

Bennett and Lotus trace our roots and our desire for liberty and individualism back before 1776 to the Anglo-Saxon invaders after the fall of the Roman Empire. Our culture has two thousand years of history, and our desire for liberty is inherited. One thing that scholars see as a sign of progress is the nuclear family with individuals, not parents, selecting their spouse. The beginning of freedom for women began when this happened, and children left their parents' home and no longer belonged to extended families. From there, they made their own wealth and expanded the economic pie.

The nuclear family encouraged the market economy and property ownership to go with common law that moved toward court cases that broke from more rigid Roman rules. America 1.0 had a decentralized government with states largely left to pursue their policies. This model came apart during the Civil War and the subsequent development of the industrial state. Economic innovation fostered growth. Big corporations rose and with it big government to counter the influence of those large corporations.

The two world wars and the Great Depression led to the formation of the bureaucratic state and the era after post-World War II from 1940s to the present stage and the 1960s was the peak of "America 2.0." America 2.0's development of the bureaucratic state has led to our present situation as we are witnessing bureaucracy on steroids. The 1980s and 1990s saw reform of the bureaucratic state that worked, but this century saw bloated government and unsustainable debt, making the demise of America 2.0 possible.

The question is whether we can move to an America 3.0 without a complete collapse, and the authors say yes, it can happen. They present a libertarian vision that includes the elimination of the federal income tax and dramatically reducing federal government power, but they still support a defensive posture that includes maintaining our present alliances, along with federal protection for civil rights. So while the authors questioned much of our foreign policy for the past decade and their criticism was similar to Trump's own message, they don't call for the non-interventionist policy of Ron Paul or his son, Rand Paul (although Rand Paul might want to adopt their policies as his own). They believe America should continue to protect the trading routes, following a policy that Britain and America have done for three centuries.

On domestic policy, they see many of our social problems being created by the Federal government and foreseeing many states forming regional compacts on policies like health care. While many conservatives and libertarians may not agree with their vision, Bennett and Lotus present a confident future for conservatives and libertarians to consider while putting together a governing vision that can unite the two groups. It is a vision that can form a basis to counter the leftist vision that governs America today.

Bennett's and Lotus's vision depends how intelligent policymakers can become. Here is the crux of their argument: the end of the present bureaucratic state can be a blessing in disguise and that America will come out of the present implosion of command-and-control bureaucracy as stronger as and more prosperous than before. The authors are happy warriors who view America's best days ahead of us.

National Review editor Ramesh Ponnuru calls this alliance of English-speaking nations, "The Empire of Freedom"[81] which he says where the United States belongs. James Bennett has termed this alliance as the

Anglosphere. Anglosphere is the branch of Western civilization that is moving beyond the West and on to its own sphere of influence. As Ponnuru writes, the Anglosphere is "no longer purely Western civilization."[82]

Bennett writes that the Anglosphere is *"Western in origin but no longer entirely Western in composition and nature, this civilization is marked by a particularly strong civil society, which is the source of its long record of successful constitutional government and economic prosperity."* [83] While European are attempting to build a European Union that is bureaucratic in nature, the Anglosphere nations are for most part suspicious of such super state institutions build from top down and instead as Bennett states, "promote more and stronger cooperative institutions, not to build some English-speaking super state on the European Union, or to annex Britain, Canada or Australia to the United States but rather to protect the English speaking nations' common values from external and internal fantasies." [84] Brexit gives us the first opening to build the Anglosphere and tie Great Britain to the United States and move away from the bureaucratic European Union, which may be beginning its own implosion.

Who is part of the Anglosphere? Author James Bennett answers, *"Geographically, the densest nodes of the Anglosphere are found in the United States and Great Britain, while Anglosphere regions of Canada, Australia, New Zealand, Ireland, and South Africa are powerful and populous outliers. The educated English-speaking populations of the Caribbean, Oceania, Africa and India constitute the Anglosphere's frontiers."* [85]

What we may be witnessing is a cooperative alliance based on defense alliances and trade. Ramesh Ponnuru notes, "An *important point here is that all these countries remain broadly in harmony on the subject of global free trade and more supportive harmony on the subject of global free trade, and more supportive of free trade than most countries outside the Anglosphere."* [86]

(We could easily see an expansion of an Anglosphere trading zone beginning with the United States and Great Britain and including Australia, New Zealand, and Canada.)

Anglosphere may be just another word for an American-led Empire of Liberty. While some feel that Europe is going in one direction and United States and other Anglosphere nations another direction, Ponnuru notes, *"Is it inconceivable that the political cultures of France and Germany could change into a free-market and pro-American direction in 20 years- or even ten?* [87]

"As Ponnuru observed, Ireland has become an economic dynamo based on free market ideals, so Europe is not yet lost to statis and it will be curious about how the rise of populism in Europe will affect all of this. European populists have less support for free markets than the Anglosphere populists but European populists don't have any real love for the European Union so who knows how this will turnout. In France, the main battle may be between the hard-core nationalist populism of Marie Le Pen and the more conservative reformist populism of Francis Fillon. (The rise of Macron is temporary victory for the EU establishment within France but his victory was due as much to French's voters' fear of Le Pen than affirmation of Macron.) While the European experience is different from North America, there is still enough similarity between the two separate cultures to make comparisons possible.

Former Margaret Thatcher advisor John O'Sullivan has called for an American policy that is pro-American while undermining the super state structure of the European Union. The present German government has is attempting to use the European Union as a tool for its own economic hegemony over Europe. Germany needs to tie Central Europe to modern Europe and many Central Europeans want an American presence in Europe to safeguard their security, not just from the European Union dominated by Germany but a resurgent Russia to their East.

James C. Bennett's thesis begins with the premise that manufacturing supremacy begins with those countries with the best information technology. Bennett notes, *"The United States, being the current leader in information technology while still possessing a large manufacturing base, is likely to be the primary beneficiary of this process."* [88] While critics have expressed concern that we are seeing an outflow of manufacturing jobs overseas, Bennett considers such observation misplaced. Bennett quips, *"This is like fearing that the advent of steel-hulled warships in the nineteenth century would undercut British or American naval might, because it made irrelevant those nations' mastery of wooden ship technology."* [89]

The dominant economic activity in the world will be information based and Bennett states that this is economic development that is moving beyond the corporate model that has dominated the nineteenth and twentieth centuries. The new economic model will feature organizations that link entrepreneur, financiers and marketers. Those nations that encourage entrepreneurship will predominate and the Anglosphere world leads in that area.

America still leads the world in the second decade of the new century. But there is a new movement of nations that is challenging America's lead, beginning with China in the Western Pacific and Russia throughout Europe and the Middle East.

In the nations that form the Anglosphere, Bennett notes, "*The market economy is more than the absence of socialism. It is more than the absence of interventionist government; it is the economic expression of a strong civil society, just as substantive democracy is the political expression of a civil society and civic state.*" [90] While there is no rule that democracy and the market economy need to exist side by side, but they often do. What matters is a civil society and understanding that government is but one player in society and part of a greater society. Religion, private charities, and corporations of varied sizes as well as political parties are all players in society that interact with one another. A strong civil society sees individuals creating and working in a variety of enterprises.

For the Anglosphere nations, strong civic societies had their roots in medieval Europe. James C. Bennett contends that in the Middle Ages, particularly in England, the modern-day society was built upon mix of "tribal, feudal, local, church family and state institutions" [91] and the lack of a single overwhelming power capable of dominating. From the Magna Carta, English princes and barons made it clear to the royal crown that they had rights and this ideal became rooted in English custom and eventually making its way across the Atlantic. When civic society is strong, government can be limited to specific duties since welfare can be provided through the private aid as well as public aid.

The weakness of the non-English-speaking nations is not the lack of creativity on the part of their people but the political institutions in place retard growth. Even in older European countries such as France and Germany, entrepreneurs are frustrated by bureaucratic inertia. And as James C. Bennett notes, *"It is likely that the Anglosphere will continue to pull away from Continental Europe and Japan."* [92] In the United States, the Obama administration placed countless obstacles in the path of economic growth. Trump's policies have much to offer as far as growth but it is possible that the Trump administration will put their own restrictions to growth through protectionist trade policies.

The United States and the United Kingdom have the world's best navies and their armed forces can operate worldwide for an extended period of time. This allows the Anglosphere to operate in any theater of the world and deploy an appropriate military response to defend their interests. Throughout the world, there are Anglosphere nations at key junctions. Australia faces a long-term serious threat in Southeast Asia as they are near heavily populated and underdeveloped Asian nations. The United States has bases throughout the world but in a world of shifting alliances and changing world crises from the Far East to the Middle East, a strong Anglosphere alliance will give Americans dependable and capable allies in crucial areas.

The British armed forces are capable of working with American military and are probably the only European nation that has the ability to operate with the technically advanced American armed forces. Australia provides an Anglosphere armed force that can also be incorporated into a strike force in key areas in the Middle East and the Far East. The Gulf War and the Iraq War showed that today the Anglosphere is the dominant military power but that the Anglosphere needs to expand the alliance, as the limits on resources are starting to appear.

James C. Bennett writes, "*The United States is facing pressure to reduce the universality of its commitments, combined with a certain fatigue among the populace for the extensive nature of American alliances… Unlike the United States, the United Kingdom has already reached the point where it is greatly limited in its ability to go it alone on any major military commitment; its armed forces are explicitly in existence to serve as leverage in a variety of alliance situations.*"[93] Bennett correctly assumes that any primary alliance should focus on nations that have strong shared values and the Anglosphere has just an alliance in place.

Indian writer Pramit Pal Chaudhuri wrote in India's *Hindustan Times* in 2003, "*Russia provides the type of weapons needed for mass wars of millions of men, thousands of warplanes and tanks. What New Delhi is looking for today is smart weaponry, stuff that will allow it to attack a terrorist camp with smart missiles or stealth-drop commandos. This is exactly what Russia cannot provide. As it is, even the warplanes it sells now have to get their more advanced avionics and missiles from Israel or France."* [94] Many nations are reexamining their military strategy and the weapons that go with it. Countries like India, Russia, and China are now studying our tactics to adopt for their own forces. The Anglosphere superiority in technology allows them to be able to fight any kind of war in any place of the world. While the rest of the world is enhancing their technology to catch up the United States, the U.S.'s commitment in various wars throughout the Middle East is taking resources away from improving our own weapon systems to stay ahead of our potential competitors.

The Iraq War and subsequent combat showed the flexibility of the American forces. The United States military won the ground war in Iraq and George W. Bush handed Barack Obama victory on the ground. Obama's diplomacy turned that victory into defeat and chaos.

What was seen during the Iraq War is that the present-day American military can now fight any style of combat. While one Russian observer stated that Americans were cowards depending solely on technology and did not like to fight street-to-street, this war proved that the Americans, borrowing from their British allies, learned street fighting. They did the dirty work while losing very few men. Contrast this to the Russians, where 50,000 people may have died in the Chechen wars during the 1990s including 5,000 Russian soldiers in similar urban combat. The British and Americans showed that one could fight in an urban environment without destroying everything and still secure the major centers. As George Patton once said, "No dumb bastard ever won a war by going out and dying for his country. He won it by making some other dumb bastard die for his country."[95] Americans and the British can fight in the urban center, in open ground, and on the sea as well as the air.

Vladimir Dvorkin, the head of the Russian Defense Ministry's think tank, reflected the thinking of many in the Russian military when he said in 1997, *"The gap between our capabilities and those of the Americans has been revealed, and it is vast. We are very lucky that Russia has no major enemies at the moment, but the future is impossible to predict, and we must be ready."* [96]

Israeli defense officials expressed similar amazement in 2003 when they witnessed one of the more powerful Arab countries conquered by what amounted to fewer than three American divisions. Major General Dan Harel told a reporter that he was jealous of the American military. He said, *"They have advanced in areas that we were leading in only a few years ago. They have the ability to put everything together in command and control. Our navy and air force have systems. But we have to integrate them."* [97] Israelis were impressed that the Americans lost slightly more than 100 men in the Gulf War whereas the Israelis lost six times as many in the Six-Day War. Both friend and foe will study the Gulf War for its appropriate lessons. Even the subsequent Iraq War has seen Allied casualties lower than comparable wars while inflicting higher causalities upon the terrorist thugs they are fighting.

What the Americans do have is ingenuity. Stephen Ambrose in his many books on World War II continuously observed that under the strain of combat, the American soldiers who were raised in freedom were constantly were able to adapt more freely to conditions on the ground than their inflexible German counterparts. Technology is not all that wins wars. It also takes the soldier on the ground to make it work. The American soldier is raised in a world of technology, so a strategy based on technology is second nature and this shows in combat as well. The American soldier brings this strength into battle.

Fred Kaplan details that the origin of the victories in the Gulf War and the Iraq War began in the early 1980s. With the advent of digital technology, a new war-fighting doctrine was born. With the defeat suffered in Vietnam, a whole generation of officers determined never to repeat Vietnam's mistakes. Among those were Huba Wass de Czege, who wrote a major revision that broke the Army's previous strategy of attrition warfare, setting up static lines against the enemy's assault, and repulsing it with superior firepower. De Czege began a new strategy that emphasizes lightning strikes behind enemy lines and emphasizing speed. Speed Kills. When the Gulf War began in 1991, many of De Czege's students were part of Norman Schwarzkopf's staff and the Gulf War was a combination of superior firepower matched with feints and the classic deep strike behind Saddam's army, still in Kuwait.

With the advent of smart bombs and their increased use in combat, the military could better target its weapons while employing deception. Increased accuracy also meant less civilian casualties. Fred Kaplan said of this strategy, *"Operation Desert Storm was really two wars—the air war and the ground war—each fought autonomously and in sequence. Gulf War II was an integrated war, waged simultaneously and in synchronicity, on the ground, at sea, and in the air. The vast majority of air strikes, from Air Force bombers and attack planes as well as Navy fighters, were delivered on Iraqi Republican Guards, in order to ease the path of U.S. Army soldiers and Marines thrusting north to Baghdad.*[98] As mentioned previously, synergy of all of the services became a reality.

In addition, Fred Kaplan stated, *"Another new thing, which started in Afghanistan and continued in Iraq, was the systematic inclusion of the so-called "shadow soldiers," the special operations forces. The 1986 Goldwater-Nichols Act, which was best-known for giving new authority to the chairman of the Joint Chiefs of Staff, also made special ops a separate command, with its own budget."*[99] The warriors of the night became an integral part of American strategy.

A pundit recently pointed out that an army that combines the use of dolphins and satellites is a tough army to beat. This is an army that is capable of using what is available to fight. Americans use old-fashioned "Yankee know-how" in war as effectively as they do in business. The entrepreneurial spirit that exists outside the military has now made its way into the military. The Anglosphere nations' power lies not just in its economic prowess but it's military as well.

What the Iraq War showed is that future wars on terrorism will be fought with actual combat, imaginative diplomacy, and through subversion of terrorist sponsor states. The combat tactics of the Iraq War demonstrated that the United States has the capability to either strike with the thunder of armed columns or special ops operating in the shadows. To win the war on terror in this century we will need armed forces that can fight under any and all conditions. Nothing replaces a well-trained soldier carrying out the policies of diplomats; but without the soldier, diplomacy is nothing more than an empty bluff. This is something the Trump administration needs to learn and the Obama administration never did learn.

The Rule of Law and Anglosphere

"L'Angleterre, en effet, est insulaire, maritime, liee par ses echanges, ses marches, son ravitaillement, aux pays les plus divers et souvent les plus lointains".[100] (England is indeed insular, maritime, and tied by its exchanges, its markets, its supply with the most diverse and often most remote countries.)

—Charles de Gaulle,
vetoing British membership
in the Common Market,
January 14, 1963.

The American Constitution is a document whose existence is rooted in a wider constitutional tradition derived from Britain. From the Middle Ages to the present, there is a continuity and stability that undergirds the Anglosphere. James C. Bennett observes that a business lawyer in New York would recognize the common law code of Australia or England. The lawyer would know the problems while dealing with any issues across the Pacific or Atlantic in a fellow Anglosphere nation.

The English monarch was never as absolute as his or her counterparts in continental Europe. From the Magna Carta onwards, the powers of the monarch were restricted. The belief in limited government has given Americans and the rest of the Anglosphere an advantage over their competitors. In the Anglosphere nations, entrepreneurship has flourished and spread beyond their borders. From the time of the American Revolution and development of the Constitution, the French have endured two Napoleons and five Republics. Outside of England, no European nation has had more experience with democratic rule than the United States. The development of a strong civil society and long time understanding of constitutional rule has fostered both political and economic freedom within the Anglosphere and led to its present domination throughout the world.

Within the Western traditions, there are now two competing ideas. For the French, there is a continental system that features extensive government intervention within the economic sphere and beyond. Many French have derided what they call "Anglo-Saxon" Ideas. In the 1960s, de Gaulle envisioned a block of nations as a separate world power that stood as a counter to the Soviet Empire and the American led "Anglo-Saxon Empire." Whether it is attacking American culture or complaining about America hegemony, much of the French intellectual and foreign policy apparatus viewed American ascendancy as counter to their goal of dominating Europe through the EU. France wants to become a major player on the world scene through various international bodies such as the European Union and the United Nations. For many French intellectuals, the EU represented the both the political and economic counterweight to what they view as "cowboy capitalism." (The problem is that EU and the euro aided Germany in being the dominant economic power within Europe, and it is no longer the French leading the way but they are becoming a tail wagged by the German dog.)

One of the future key issues for the Anglosphere nations will be Great Britain's relations with Europe. The present EU and continental system favors more bureaucratic control over the economy and increased industrial policies targeting specific industries. The harmonization of taxes and budgets within the EU is designed to maintain high taxes and support an ever-expanding welfare state. The policy of harmonization is being used as wedge against lower tax countries such as those in Ireland and in the emerging democracies in Central Europe. Britain's goal of being "the Anglosphere voice" would have been compromised by dealings with the French and Germans, the present leaders of the EU. James C. Bennett observed in 2007, "Were the United Kingdom to leave the Union and join NAFTA, it would lead to far more productive partnership." [101]

For Bennett, Britain needs to be more closely integrated into the Anglosphere through inclusion in NAFTA and the other Anglosphere pacts. This is a more logical alliance as Bennett observed that having the

United Kingdom join NAFTA would, "accelerate the existing trend toward mergers, partnerships, and alliances between U.S., Canadian, and British infotech companies. It would extend them into allied defense and defense-impacted fields such as aerospace and commercial aviation." [102] In other words, Brexit.

Many European leaders have learned the wrong lessons of the past fifty years. At this moment, Europe is at peace for the first time in a millennium but with the resurgence of Putin's Russia, there exists for the first time a prospect of a major European war. This peace came as a result of American steadfast military support of Western Europe. During the 2016 campaign, Trump refuse to committing American support for NATO and European collective security.

India and the Anglosphere

James C. Bennett does not yet consider India formally part of the Anglosphere but for the Anglosphere to dominate the 21st century, India must become part of the alliance. He writes, *"In such a commonwealth (Anglosphere), should the Indian choose to engage it, It may well be that Bangalore becomes a major center of the Anglosphere in thirty or fifty years' time. Anglospherists do not fear this, knowing that just as London is still great today because it shares an Anglosphere with New York and Los Angeles, it and the American metropolises will be great tomorrow partly because they might share it with Bangalore."* [103]

Indian writer Gurcharan Das remembers attending Henry Kissinger's lectures at Harvard in the early 1960s and listening to Kissinger point out that Nehru was a dreamer and "it is dangerous to put dreamers in power."[104] Kissinger's own views on Nehru may have been misplaced and he admitted it in his most recent book on diplomacy. Nehru was not an idealist and certainly not a pacifist like Gandhi. When force was needed, Nehru was prepared to use it. Three wars with Pakistan, including the liberation of Bangladesh from Pakistan in 1971, one war with China, and pushing the Portuguese out of Goa showed that India was not afraid of using military force. What Kissinger called a foreign policy of dreamers was a serious attempt to buy time for the new nation, residing as it does in a tough neighborhood. Kissinger's own opinion from his Harvard days changed when he stated *"India's conduct during the Cold War was not so different from that of the United States in its formative decades."* [105] The difference is that in the United States' formative years, there was an ocean between America and Europe. India, on the other hand, is in a region populated by vipers and political rivals.

The United States, as the leader of NATO and the premier Western power, has inherited the traditional British interest in ensuring that no one single nation dominates the Eurasia landmass. India, also, has co-opted policy from its former English master. In 1934 Britain designed a plan to stabilize the Sino-India border and to dominate the Indian Ocean from Aden to Singapore. India's present naval building effort reflects those same objectives. Like the United States, India does not want to see an Islamic fundamentalist revolution sweep through the Middle East. As China grows in strength and challenges the United States in the Far East, China also threatens India at her northern borders and through the sea lanes including the Indian Ocean.

A recent stumbling block that stood in the way of Indian-American relations was India's ownership of the bomb. Kissinger noted that India "will not risk it' survival *"on exhortations coming from countries basing their own security on nuclear weapons."*[106] Kissinger concedes that India is acting rationally and that President Clinton's reaction to India's holding nuclear tests in 1998 and subsequent expansion of its nuclear capacities was "emotional."[107] While Clinton would tell the Indians that they did not need nuclear weapons, India's own reaction was to ignore Clinton's appeal. As far as Indians were concerned, they were not under the American nuclear umbrella and were facing two nuclear rivals, Pakistan and China, in their own backyard. The Bush Administration removed the various sanctions put in place in 1998 after the events of September 11.

The biggest problem with nuclear non-proliferation is the unrealistic approach that good intentions are enough to ensure enforcement. The 1994 Nuclear Proliferation Prevention Act requires the imposition of sanctions against any nation that pursues and acquires nuclear weapons. These sanctions include denial of World Bank aid, restricting bank loans and technology exports. The problem with this approach is that it does not distinguish between friend and foe. India's nuclear program is designed to protect against growing Chinese military clout, and the desire to counter Pakistan's intentions in South Asia. Nuclear weapons are India's entry into the superpower club and India's nuclear plan does not threaten America. New Delhi's actions are not motivated by any desire for a military confrontation with the United States, now or in the future. Washington has tolerated nuclear weapons in the hands of the U.S.S.R. and Red China, so why not India? India's nuclear possession does not threaten American interests any more than do France and England with their nuclear capability.

France's own nuclear plan was based simply on the idea that France and only France is responsible for its own security. England also did not choose to live strictly under America's nuclear umbrella and India is merely following its own national interest in becoming a nuclear power. If anything, Obama's own policy led to nuclear proliferation. When Obama and Hillary Clinton led the effort to overthrow Gaddafi in 2011, they increased the chances of nuclear proliferation since Gaddafi surrendered his own weapons of mass destruction in exchange for neutrality in the war on terror. The message to any future nation with nuclear weapons that to trade them in exchange for American security is riskier than keeping the weapons. Ukraine's own security was also guaranteed by both Russia and United States when they gave up nuclear weapons on their border. Today, Putin controls a third of Ukraine through proxies, and annexed the Crimea. If our allies can't trust our own nuclear umbrella, they will obtain their own nuclear weapons. Does anyone think that Saudi Arabia won't obtain their own nuclear weapons if Iran finally obtains its bomb?

The final solution is simply the adoption of the Strategic Defense Initiative. The use of technology to checkmate present missile technology allows the United States and her allies, including India, to maintain its military superiority while giving potential nuclear powers a reason not to proceed with their own program. SDI provides the West an insurance policy against any cheaters. The days of depending upon mere pieces of papers for security are over. A missile shield allows the United States to protect its own national interest, while securing a nuclear umbrella to protect other nations, including India. The reason that the nuclear club has not gotten even bigger is that America's nuclear umbrella has been extended to potential nuclear powers such as Japan and Germany, and in the past there was no need for those countries to be nuclear powers in their own right as long as they are allied with the United States. (The Obama administration's reckless policies that rewarded our enemies more than our allies will only encourage many of these allies to pursue their own nuclear weapons to ensure their own defense.) A strategic defense initiative protects the United States in a world of changing alliances. China has made it clear that it is considering challenging the United States' role in East Asia and its own nuclear and military buildup is predicated upon its own military objectives that are not necessarily in sync with ours. SDI allows a sensible policy of containment if that is what is required in the future, and also allows for reduction in nuclear weapons since it allows nations an insurance policy against cheating and reduces the utilities of nuclear weapons.

A new nuclear non-proliferation policy begins with the principle that we can no longer keep the nuclear genie in the bottle. There are some nations in whose hands nuclear weapons may in fact be a stabilizing factor. In the 19th century, Europe was dominated by a concert of leading powers, whose goal was to maintain the peace and European stability after the end of the Napoleonic wars. What is required today is a concert of democratic states, starting with the Anglosphere and including other democratic states like India. In this new era of terror, stability is dependent upon this new group of nations acting in harmony. And certainly, this concert of power should include other alliances with other nations not just limited to the Anglosphere. While military options will always be considered, the ultimate protection is a new group of democratic states prepared to defend what is right under the umbrella of a Strategic Defense Initiative and backed by the United States-led Anglosphere.

The final piece to India's greatness will be the evolution of its relationship with Pakistan, including how it deals with the Kashmir question. Pakistan, formed as a result of the partition of 1947, has been a dysfunctional society, cash strapped and living in the shadow of India. For millions of Indians and Pakistanis, the partition had its own human tragedy, ending in the deaths of hundreds of thousands, if not millions. Pakistan's former strongman, Pervez Musharraf, migrated from his home in India to Pakistan after partition, whereas author and business consultant Gurcharan Das went in the opposite direction as a refugee. Nearly 40 million people traveled in either direction in a tragedy that today still threatens both the security and prosperity of India and Pakistan. India diverts billions of dollars of defense funds that should go into economic development and expanding its own influence outside the South Asia continent to defending its borders with Pakistan. As for Kashmir, Pakistan's claim is due to a substantial Muslim population, and some in Pakistan even view Kashmir as a part of a "Greater Pakistan." India views Kashmir as part of its own territory and the Kashmiri people, themselves, are uncertain about their own fate.

A democratic, moderate Pakistan would be a boon to peace in the region and possibly give India an extra market for their products. India is now the dominant power on the South Asian continent. An autocratic, economically dysfunctional Pakistan is not in the interest of either the United States or India. Pakistan stands between the forces of Islamic radicalism and modernity and is proving to be a dysfunctional nation.

Great Britain was the inspiration for both the United States and India in the values of freedom. Both nations now have the responsibility to spread those values throughout the world. A country of more than a billion people will never be a junior partner in any relationship and, unlike Great Britain, India will be an equal partner based on its potential as an economic and nuclear power. With nearly a million Indians living throughout the United States, there is a personal connection being developed between these two nations. These immigrants live in America but much of their heart belongs to India. These people to people contacts further cement relations between these countries. These contacts also bring down the veil between these countries as well. As India learns more about the United States, we also learn more about India.

India will prove useful in battling terrorists and defending the West. India, for many years, has set itself apart from the West, but in recent years, this is beginning to change. Gone are the days of reflective anti-American attitudes that infiltrated Indian leadership and there is a more balanced approach to world events. It will be imperative among American policy makers to encourage India to become a permanent member of the Anglosphere

SDI and Anglosphere Technical Superiority

I
n 1988, I managed the campaign of GOP candidate Mary Ellen Lobb, who was running against Democrat incumbent Alan Wheat in Missouri's 5th District. One of the issues that we highlighted was Ronald Reagan's Strategic Defense Initiative. When discussing SDI, Lobb told me that "we must remind the voters that within the next decade, we'll need strategic defense not just against the Soviet Empire but various Third World regional powers such as Iran." We would not always be in a world, separated into two armed camps led by the Soviet Union and the United States.

Within a year after the election, the world that Mary Ellen Lobb foresaw became a reality. The Berlin Wall fell and the Soviet Empire imploded. In this century, we've seen the rise of regional powers that threaten our own national interests-including Iran in the Middle East and China in the Far East. Missile technology is no longer "high technology", and it is spreading to rogue nations such as North Korea, making them become "superpowers" on the cheap.

In the 19th century, Great Britain was the dominant world power based on her navy, which allowed the English to project force throughout the globe. England maintained bases on every continent to defend the empire. Britain's population was relatively small, precluding a dominant standing army, and her statesmen understood that her superpower status was delicately poised. British defense plans were based on maintaining naval superiority supplemented by continental alliances against whatever nation was threatening to dominate Europe.

When Kaiser Wilhelm II decided to challenge British naval hegemony, English statesmen took this as a challenge to British world dominance. Throughout the 19th century, Great Britain maintained technical superiority over all opponents, taking advantage of its industrial might as the world's strongest and freest economy. This allowed Great Britain to maintain its military superiority.

The collapse of the British Empire after World War II ended the British domination in world affairs. The United States, through the Marshall Plan and the GATT system of trade, inherited England's mantle as the defender of Western democracy while the Soviet Empire assumed Hitler's role as the exemplar of socialism. The Soviet Union dominated the Eurasian landmass, with the largest standing army in history and by the time Ronald Reagan became President, the Soviet Empire stretched from the Berlin Wall to the Pacific Ocean, with satellite nations on every inhabited continent, including North Vietnam, Angola, Ethiopia, Cuba, and Nicaragua. The threat it posed was real.

The Cold War ended with a whimper, not a bang, as the Soviet command economy collapsed. This felicitous outcome was due in part to the Reagan administration's military buildup and the beginning of the SDI program. The Soviet economy could not compete with technological advances that a free economy adapted to military use. The West's superiority in military hardware was showcased during the Gulf and Iraq Wars. These conflicts also illustrated the security threats of this century. Iraq, a regional power, launched Scud missiles against our allies throughout the Gulf War. As Patriot missiles dueled Scuds, we saw the first field demonstration of why strategic defense is essential. In the Gulf War, this missile duel was a sideshow. In a future regional conflict, it may become the main event, whether the payloads are nuclear, chemical, or biological.

The major impediment to missile defense is not technology, but America's will to deploy. As Professor Frederick Seitz, a leading expert in missile technology, concluded, *"The science behind missile defense is solid, and we certainly do possess the capabilities to defend ourselves."* Seitz observes that missile defense technology has been around for decades. The key to its success today is the ability to destroy enemy missiles in their boost phase, when decoys can be more readily defeated. The difficulties of boost-phase intercept are best approached through space-based and naval platform systems. With the demise of the ABM treaty, the last legal restraint to develop these systems has been removed.

American missile defense allows Americans to protect potential land-based allies, freeing them to divert their energies toward trade, currency reform, and capital formation. Pax Americana-—the extension of democracy and economic development throughout the Third World—depends on America's ability to prevent aggressive regional powers from becoming international powers "on the cheap." Strategic defense is a key component of this strategy. The sea-based Aegis missile extends a defensive shield to our allies, and expands our naval superiority over any potential enemies. A space-based anti-missile capability ensures the defense of our key command centers in space and allows protection of the American people. With our technical superiority, we will be able to neutralize the nuclear capabilities of most regional powers such as Iran and China. SDI is a manifestation of the Anglosphere's technical superiority.

During the 20th century, the United States became the dominant superpower. SDI will allow America and the Anglosphere to continue to exert its influence throughout the world-, with the result being an expansion of economic and political freedom, worldwide. The United States is a commercial nation similar to nineteenth-century Britain, and depends upon the freedom of voluntary commerce to ensure its economic well-being. NATO was an established land-based alliance to ensure that no power dominates the Eurasian continent and this ensured the general peace of Europe. Now NATO cohesion is now threatened and in the United States, support for NATO is on the wane and it may be on the wane within Europe as well.

Trump: The Beginning of Realpolitik

Trump's foreign policy may be a return to the *realpolitik* of the Nixon era and Trump's foreign policy may have a coherent strategy based on a balance of power view of the world. Michael Barone noted, *"Some will dismiss his appointments and tweets as expressing no more than the impulses of an ignorant and undisciplined temperament — no more premeditated than the lunges of a rattlesnake. Others may recall that similar things were said (by me, as well as many others) about his campaign strategy. But examination of the entrails of the election returns suggests that Trump was following a deliberate strategy based on shrewd insight when he risked antagonizing white college-educated voters in the process of appealing to non-college-educated whites."* 108

Historian Niall Ferguson views Trump's foreign policy as an extension of Henry Kissinger's worldview. He observed, *"A world run by regional great powers with strong men in command, all of whom understand that any lasting international order must be based on the balance of power."* 109

As Michael Barone notes, Trump took a congratulatory call for his election victory from Taiwan's president. The first visitor to Trump Tower after the election was Japanese Prime Minister Shinzo Abe; this sent a message that China will not be allowed to operate in the Western Pacific unchallenged and Trump will work with our allies. Trump also appointed Terry Branstad the governor of Iowa, as the ambassador to China. Branstad first met Xi Jinping in 1985. Barone views the appointment as a "bad cop, good cop" move. He observed, *"Trump wants some changes in trade relations with China and limits on its probes in the South China Sea and will build up U.S. military forces. But there's room for acceptance of China as a great power. Trump wants some changes in trade relations with China and limits on its probes in the South China Sea and will build up U.S. military forces."* 110

As for dealing with Russia, Barone added, *"There's room for acceptance of Russia, too, as suggested by the secretary-of-state nomination of Exxon Mobil CEO Rex Tillerson, self-proclaimed friend of Russian president Vladimir Putin's. He may be opposed by Republican senators who, like Mitt Romney in 2012, see Russia as "our No. 1 geopolitical foe." But perhaps Trump favors Kissinger's proposal for a neutral and decentralized (i.e., dominated and partitioned) Ukraine, with an end to sanctions on Russia. Tillerson would be a good choice if that were your goal. This would make the Baltic States and Poland understandably nervous, but they could take some comfort in Trump's reaffirmation of our NATO pledge to defend them and in the fact that Pentagon nominee James Mattis has gone out of his way to honor Estonia for its sacrifices in Iraq and Afghanistan."* [111]

Trump's criticism of NATO, including that NATO member states should contribute more toward their own defenses, may have seen results. As Michael Barone noted, *"Finance ministers, stung by Trump's campaign criticisms, are ponying up more money to meet their NATO defense-spending commitments; German chancellor Angela Merkel is backing down from her disastrous decision to welcome 1 million refugees."* [112]

Brexit was the first break in the European Union's dominance of the continent. While Obama threatened Britain with being sent to the "back of the queue" if they voted to leave the EU, Trump supported Brexit and the U.S-U.K. free trade agreement. Brexit could be the first step toward the formation of the Anglosphere. Trump, as part of his "America First" foreign policy, has little use for multinational organizations. The Anglosphere is an alliance that supports Trump's view of America's new role in the world.

In the Middle East, will Trump ditch the Iranian deal or police it more aggressively? Will he booster the Sunni-Israeli alliance against increasing Iranian influence? Trump's choices may reflect accommodation toward this strategy. While Trump may pay less lip service to human rights, the reality is that Obama also paid lip service to human rights.

Niall Ferguson noted, *"Yet it was Trump who in August pledged that his Administration would "speak out against the oppression of women, gays and people of different faith" in the name of Islam. While the Obama Administration has shunned proponents of Islamic reform, Trump pledged to "be a friend to all moderate Muslim reformers in the Middle East, and [to] amplify their voices. This includes speaking out against the horrible practice of honor killings," as well as establishing as "one of my first acts as President...*

a Commission on Radical Islam which will include reformist voices in the Muslim community." [113]

Ferguson's point is that Trump may not make human rights a central theme of his foreign policy but he may be more willing to stand up for those rights in his own way. President Obama often talked the importance of human rights, but the Obama administration often ignored people who were truly suffering. His Syria policy may be responsible for the death of a half million Syrians, not to mention the thousands of people who died in Iraq and other Middle East nations as a result of Obama's reckless policies.

Trump's screening of would-be immigrants for links not just to terrorism but also to a political Islam that promotes a sharia law inconsistent with our Constitution is similar to measures taken during the Cold War excluding communists. Ferguson compared Trump's foreign policy to Theodore Roosevelt's. He wrote, *"It is also precisely the way Theodore Roosevelt spoke when anarchists posed a threat to American values. After all, Roosevelt became President only because the anarchist Leon Czolgosz murdered President William McKinley in September 1901, and Roosevelt himself narrowly avoided assassination in 1912."* [114] Trump views radical Jihadism as more an ideology than a religion, which leads to his view about restricting Muslim immigration.

Theodore Roosevelt condemned anarchism in his first annual address to Congress in the terrorist ideology, *"[T]he teachings of professed anarchists, and probably also by the reckless utterances of those who on the stump and in the public press, appeal to the dark and evil spirits of malice and greed, envy and sullen hatred. The wind is sowed by the men who preach such doctrines, and they cannot escape their share of responsibility for the whirlwind that is reaped. . . . The man who advocates anarchy directly or indirectly, in any shape or fashion, or the man who apologizes for anarchists and their deeds, makes himself morally accessory to murder before the fact."* [115]

Roosevelt wanted to exclude and deport anarchists, and Congress agreed by passing laws that did exactly that. Niall Ferguson compared Roosevelt's speech with Trump's views, *"Today, for anarchism read radical Islam."* [116]

In 1982, Herman Kahn wrote *The Coming Boom*, in which he foresaw the economic prosperity of the Reagan years and a new world order that included the rise of regional powers and new challenges to the bipolar power struggle between the United States and the U.S.S.R. Kahn thought that a multipolar world would eventually stabilize but the era before stabilization could be chaotic. Kahn's predictions proved to be accurate.

Kahn saw the rise of China, Japan, and Germany as powers. Today, Germany is the leading European economic power and Russia is working on expanding its sphere of influence within Central Europe while reestablishing Russian nationalism. China is working on being a Pacific power and both Russia and China look to put checks on American power. After the collapse of the Soviet Empire, United States was the lone superpower but Russia, China, Germany, and India are now looking for their own place as global powers. The rise of these countries signifies that we live in a multipolar world.

The Trump Administration will challenge our loyalty to transnational organizations, beginning with the United Nations. If one is serious about foreign policy, you can't be serious about the United Nations, but if you are serious about the United Nations, you can't be serious about foreign policy. When Obama failed to veto a UN resolution condemning Israel after the 2016 election, this reminded many Americans and most Republicans of the anti-American and anti-Israeli attitude of much of the United Nations.

Lawrence Sondhaus in his book *World War One: The Global Revolution* discussed the debate about the U.S. joining the League of Nations and how the Republicans in the Senate failed to ratify Woodrow Wilson's vision of transnational collective security. Sondhaus observed that while Henry Cabot Lodge opposed the League of Nations, he favored an active foreign policy that defended American interests similar to what President Theodore Roosevelt followed during his administration. Lodge supported a separate treaty that promised France that the United States and Great Britain would defend her, since Lodge perceived this treaty as being in our national interest. Wilson's refusal to separate the debate over whether America should join the League of Nations from the issue of America signing the Versailles Treaty doomed United States support for the Versailles Treaty. A similar debate will soon begin about America's involvement in transnational organizations such as the United Nations and whether it is in our national interest to stay in or at least be as active in these organizations as in the past. Trump's "America first" foreign policy doesn't mean isolationism, but a foreign policy that defends America's interest first.

Anne Bayefsky, director of the Touro Institute for Human Rights and the Holocaust, stated about the UN resolutions about Israel, "Let's be absolutely clear about what has just happened. *The Palestinians have completed the hijacking of every major UN institution. The 2016 General Assembly has adopted nineteen resolutions condemning Israel and nine critical of all other UN states combined. The 2016 Commission on the Status of Women adopted one resolution condemning Israel and zero on any other state. The 2016 UN Human Rights Council celebrated ten years of adopting more resolutions and decisions condemning Israel than any other place on earth. And now — to the applause of the assembled — the Palestinians can add the UN Security Council to their list... Resolution sponsors Malaysia and New Zealand explained UN-think to the Council this way: Israeli settlements are "the single biggest threat to peace" and the "primary threat to the viability of the two-state solution." Not seven decades of unremitting Arab terror and violent rejection of Jewish self-determination in the historic homeland of the Jewish people...At its core, this UN move is a head-on assault on American democracy. President Obama knew full well he did not have Congressional support for the Iran deal, so he went straight to the Security Council first. Likewise, he knew that there would have been overwhelming Congressional opposition to this resolution, so he carefully planned his stealth attack...He waited until Congress was not in session. Members of his administration made periodic suggestions that nothing had been decided. There were occasional head fakes that he was "leaning" against it. He produced smiling photo-ops from a Hawaiian golf course with no obvious major foreign policy moves minutes away. Holiday time-outs were in full-swing across the country. And then he pounced, giving Israel virtually no notice of his intent not to veto."* [117]

Donald Trump s bringing back *realpolitik*, in which our country's foreign policy will be based on America's national interest. Idealism will no longer be a reason to send young Americans into combat, but defending our national interest will.

Rise of Oil and Natural Gas as Our Weapon

The recent uptick in American energy production is one of those economic miracles not thought possible a decade ago. Oil and gas production will reduce the United States' dependence on imported energy, and we may be become an energy exporter, strengthening our international status. The rise of domestic energy production was done despite the Obama Administration, which tried to slow increases in oil and natural gas production.

As Manhattan Institute fellow Mark P. Mills notes, *"Growth in natural gas has made America the world's largest producer and could soon make us a huge exporter. In the past half-dozen years, America's hydrocarbon juggernaut has boosted our economy by hundreds of dollars."* [118] Mills argued noted that there are some myths about America's energy boom that need to be dispelled. One of these is that Big Oil is the biggest benefactor. He notes that 75 percent of our oil and natural gas production comes from 20,000 small and midsized oil and gas firms with an average number of 15 employees.

The oil and natural gas boom is part of a larger tech boom as it is dependent on what Mills describes as *"The emergence of information-centric 'smart' drilling, which relies on sensors, computers and control systems that, when combined with steerable horizontal drilling, fracking and a skilled work force, created the boom."* [119]

This boom has spread throughout the country. North Dakota has become a job mecca. Texas's economic growth job production has been aided by its energy industry. But jobs have been created in many states, such as Pennsylvania, Florida, Illinois, and Ohio. (New York has banned fracking and denying many New Yorkers an opportunity to profit from the fracking revolution.) California ranks behind Texas in energy production and potential. Many of these states support Democrats and this energy revolution has the potential to lift these states out of their economic doldrums. (Unfortunately, California governor Jerry Brown is determined to ensure that his state fail to develop its natural resources in favor of more expensive and less dependable green technology.)

For every energy production job created in the field, there are three or four jobs created, including information services, blue-collar jobs, and education. This has led to foreign firms investing $166 billion in American energy. More importantly, these energy-related jobs can't be exported overseas! Economic growth isn't just limited to energy production; hydrocarbon manufacturing, including petroleum refining and extraction has grown 40 percent for the past six years and these new plants have generated 600,000 jobs.

The key obstacle to this energy-related boom is federal government policy. Antiquated laws that restrict U.S. natural gas exports no longer make sense, in particular in light of the recent Russian moves threatening natural gas supplies to Central and Western Europe. These energy exports mean more jobs and more investment in the U.S. The final obstacle will be environmental extremists pushing regulations through many stats, such as the fracking bans that have taken place in New York, Maryland, and Vermont.

The energy boom is a game changer. The United States, along with Mexico and Canada, now has the potential of being the world's leading energy giant, neutralizing OPEC and allowing the United States more leeway in foreign affairs.

Where to Go on Trade

My old friend, the late Richard Nadler, reviewed the political history of trade policies from the founding of our nation through the end of the 20th century in his book on Pat Buchanan. His analysis rebuked the idea that the Founding Fathers supported protectionism.

Tariffs were the primary way that the federal government funded itself throughout much of the 19th century. They provided significant federal government revenues throughout most of our history until the Great Depression. Much of the debate around tariffs in the 19th century was similar to what we hear today about the effect of marginal tax rates among businesses and individuals today and what the proper rate is for maximum revenues.

In 1831, Albert Gallatin penned *Free Trade Memorial* as part of a free trade convention put together by John Calhoun, countering the high tariffs passed in the 1820s. The goals of the convention was to lower tariffs and flatten the rates, to accompany spending cuts to reduce the national debt. Gallatin observed, *"Moderate duties will also, as they always do, produce a greater proportionate revenue than when raised to an extravagant rate."* [120] I doubt that many supply siders would disagree with this.

(South Carolina threatened to secede over the high tariffs but a combination of Andrew Jackson threatening to hang Calhoun and others if they did secede from the Union combined with the reduction of tariffs prevented the American Civil War occurring in 1832.)

The Founding Fathers were raised in the era of the economic theories of mercantilism in which, the British government restricted the American colonies' ability to trade. In *The Wealth of Nations*, Adam Smith rejected mercantilist theory. While supporting the benefits of free trade, Smith did mention that nations could pursue tariffs in certain situations including:

National and bounties to encourage navigation and naval industries, encouraging stronger defense and aid in commerce.

Protecting infant industries with temporary assistances and bounties, with emphasis on the word "temporary."

Temporary tariffs against nations as part of a retaliation against protectionist nations, to induce those nations to change policies.

Adam Smith noted that there would be cases that imposing tariffs were a necessary evil to gain entrance to new markets, but that the goal was always to expand trade. Alexander Hamilton was a protectionist, but his protectionism was designed to help infant American industry, to provide and diversify a manufacturing base to go with America's agricultural strength. Hamilton's recommended tariff rates were significantly lower what many 19th century free traders viewed as necessary to raise revenues. Hamilton's dilemma was dealing with an American economy heavily dependent on agriculture and making it vulnerable to outside forces that could easily cut off farm exports.

Abraham Lincoln was a protectionist and during the Civil War, high tariffs were used not only to protect American industry but also to raise money for the war. We don't know if Lincoln would have lowered tariffs or maintain the high war rates to increase American industry, but Republicans did support high tariffs over the second half of the 19th century and through the first third of the 20th century.

The nation saw substantial increase in immigration levels which actually created new market or domestic home goods. As Richard Nadler noted in his book *Peril of Pat*, "You can't pick a 55-year stretch of American history and find decline." Nadler was challenging the idea that economic growth between 1860–1914 proved that protectionism was a sound policy. Productivity increased during this period as did GNP but many workers saw wage increases, compared to the liberalized trade era between World War II and the 1970s. Nor did protectionism protect American works from suffering from recessions that occurred over the last third of the 19th century.

It is difficult to draw direct economic comparisons between the last half of the 19th century and today due to productivity increases, and America's reliance on a gold standard in the 1800s. The last half of the 19th century was deflationary. While workers' incomes from 1860 through

1900 rose just 0.6 percent per year, the dollars were stronger and wages may have been higher in real terms due to the stronger value of money. The biggest losers in the last half of the 19th century were farmers who found themselves paying off their debts with stronger dollars while the actual price of their goods declined. This was good for urban workers but not good farmers, who were barely making ends meet.

The last half of the 19th century saw a debate over trade policies and monetary policies, as many in the Western United States wanted to see a more inflated currency and more access to cheaper world goods. Americans workers were able to buy more with their wages due to increased productivity and deflation, and America was becoming more urban, thus the deflation actually benefitted many of people who moved to cities. Increased immigration to the U.S. helped create a domestic market. By 1900, one third of Americans were not born in the United States but were immigrants.

The 1920s and 1930s proved to be a testing ground for what we can call "Trumponomics." When Warren G. Harding became president in 1921, the country was in a recession that was close to a depression, but the Harding administration allowed the market to heal itself, and the boom of the 1920s began.

Trade barriers remained high in the 1920s, but the Coolidge administration lowered tax rates and reduced government spending, resulting in modest income growth for workers and high GNP. So growth occurred during a period of immigration restriction and high tariffs. When the Great Depression hit in 1929 to 1930, Herbert Hoover pursued policies that were the opposite of Harding's laissez-faire cure for a troubled economy. The result was that the Great Depression became Hoover's albatross.

The lesson of the Great Depression showed the economic damage caused by high tariffs when Hoover sent rates even higher with Smoot-Hawley in 1930, arguing that it was necessary to protect jobs as a result of the 1929 downturn. Economist Thomas Sowell noted that more than a thousand economists predicted retaliations from other countries which become a reality after the passage of Smoot-Hawley. As Sowell observed, *"The unemployment rate in the United States was 6 percent in June 1930, when the Smoot-Hawley tariffs were passed—down from 8 percent in January 1930.* [121] After this tariff was passed, the unemployment jumped to 15 percent in

1931 and by the 1932 election, had risen to 26 percent. Smoot-Hawley did play a role of deepening the 1929 recession and turning it into a long term economic downturn that lasted more than a decade.

Sowell in his book *Basic Economics* explained, *"One of the most tragic examples of such restrictions occurred during the worldwide depression of the 1930s, when tariff barriers and other restrictions went up around the world. The net result was that world exports in 1933 were only one-third of what they had been in 1929.... Just as free trade provides economic benefits to all countries simultaneously, so trade restrictions reduce the efficiency of all countries simultaneously, lowering standards of living, without producing the increased employment that was hoped for."* [122]

Trump's economic plan combines traditional supply side Republican policies with a nationalistic industrial policy of rewarding Midwest manufacturing jobs. Trump former chief strategist Steve Bannon noted, *"Like [Andrew] Jackson's populism, we're going to build an entirely new political movement... It's everything related to jobs. The conservatives are going to go crazy. I'm the guy pushing a trillion-dollar infrastructure plan. With negative interest rates throughout the world, it's the greatest opportunity to rebuild everything. Shipyards, iron works, get them all jacked up. We're just going to throw it up against the wall and see if it sticks. It will be as exciting as the 1930s, greater than the Reagan revolution—conservatives, plus populists, in an economic nationalist movement."* [123]

In the 1920s, Coolidge's economic policies worked because they limited government domestic policies. But Herbert Hoover, when faced with an economic crisis, reverted to a progressive stance of using government interventionist policies, including higher taxes and more government stimulus.

Another aspect of protectionism is that many companies will set up offices in Washington to seek protection for their industries. Jay Cost in his book, *A Republic No More*, noted, *"The final policy, a strong protective tariff, was not so much an economic necessity as it was a political one. The tariff benefitted key electoral constituencies, keeping them with the GOP even if other aspects of its program did not aid them."* [124] Cost described how the political class in the 19th century intermingled with the many of the wealthy, comparable to the globalist class today.

Throughout our history, it was not uncommon for American presidents to seek temporary economic rehabilitation against other countries to open up trade opportunities for American goods and services. Both President Reagan and President George W. Bush did this, putting "tariffs" on selected goods and industries from other countries. But their goal was to liberalize trade not to restrict it, and both presidents made sure these steps were temporary, and used as a means to open up trade and reduce barriers to American goods. (There are plenty of economic studies to show that these temporary tariffs and import restrictions are counterproductive, a risk one takes in instituting temporary tariffs in order to create a more liberalized trading system.)

The Trump administration can certainly use these tactics if the goal is to liberalize trade. But as the recent Carrier episode showed, we should be leery of a president who uses his bully pulpit to threaten American corporation with consequences if they choose to move factories overseas. (Sarah Palin even condemned the Carrier deal post-election as crony capitalism.) There are two lessons to be had here. Corporate taxes matter, as companies view taxes as part of doing business and if taxes are too high; they look elsewhere. But increased regulations on business equally matter since they, too, affect the bottom line. Therefore, a good long-term strategy would be to lower corporate taxes and reduce regulations.

Trump's tax and regulatory plans recognize that dealing with the cost of doing business, including the tax and regulatory burdens imposed by government, matters. In the aftermath of the 1929 stock market crash, Herbert Hoover implored business leaders to keep wages high and production moving forward while encouraging state government to begin reconstruction. Hoover used his presidential pulpit to encourage businesses to keep production high and not lay off their workers but his policies undermined his rhetoric. If Trump enacts the right policies—and there are signs that he is willing to do that on the tax side—then his plan will succeed. The lessons of Hoover can't be ignored. Bad policies will undermine the presidential bully pulpit.

CHAPTER FIVE

What Needs to Be Done

Cruz and Rubio: Different Views on the World

If the era of Trump has delayed the Republican future, that wasn't clear during the first part of 2016. During the 2016 election, the future of conservatism was being fought between Marco Rubio and Ted Cruz. Rubio's and Cruz's families both came to America from Cuba, but even though they were both Cuban-Americans, the island hid the differences between the two and the emerging Hispanic community. Rubio, like most Hispanics, is Roman Catholic, but Cruz is Southern Baptist, and a rising number Hispanics are evangelicals. Before Rubio moved to the Senate, he was a Florida legislator including being the Speaker of the House. Cruz worked in Bush's Department of Justice and the FTC before becoming the solicitor general for Texas, which included arguing in front of the Supreme Court.

Both men would have brought more experience in actual governing than President Obama if either were elected in 2016, President Obama had a four-year Senate career, and before that was a back bencher in the Illinois legislation. Rubio was a leader in the Florida House and Cruz worked in Washington and argued some of the bigger cases drafting the amicus brief for *Heller*, a significant victory for gun rights supported by 31 state attorney generals.

The differences between the two reflected the differences within the Republican Party. Rubio's tax plan depended on tax credits for the middle class. His goal was to promote family values through the tax system. He left the top rate at 35 percent, which is only a slight drop from the present system. Ted Cruz proposed a flat 10 percent tax plus a 16 percent rate on business that similar to a value added tax. In foreign affairs, Rubio campaigned as more of an interventionist whereas Cruz's foreign policy was a return to the pre-9/11 more modest view of foreign affairs. Cruz talked of a gold standard for monetary policy; adopting aspects of the Rand Paul agenda. (Even Trump may lean toward a dollar based on the weight of gold.) This debate between Rubio and Cruz over economic policy reflects a divide among Republicans between those who view tax reform as the Holy Grail and those who viewed increasing middle-class income as the primary objective. Trump's individual tax plans are similar to Rubio's and his business plan is similar to what Cruz proposed.

Both Cruz and Rubio are social conservatives and supporters of gun rights but that is the norm for Republicans even in the era of Trump. Cruz actually argued Second Amendment cases in front of the Supreme Court and Cruz has made it clear he opposes crony capitalism including ethanol and sugar subsidies, the latter supported by Rubio. As the Carrier case in Indiana demonstrated. Trump is not above supporting his version of crony capitalism if it benefits his voters. (Florida politicians support sugar just as Iowa politicians support ethanol.)

As for Rubio, he was part of the Gang of Eight efforts for immigration reform but eventually abandoned the effort. Throughout the 2016 primaries, Rubio was persecuted for being part of the Gang of Eight and he did a rather poor job of separating himself from them. Trump was to the left of the Gang of Eight before he ran for the presidency but moved toward the restrictionist side during the primaries. On immigration, Rubio made it clear, just as Trump and Cruz have, that there will be no reforms before the borders are secured. The biggest difference between Cruz and Rubio is that Cruz will not support any path to citizenship for those who are here illegally whereas Rubio appear ready to accept a path to citizenship if certain conditions were met after a period of years. (The reality with Trump's immigration proposals is the number of illegals staying in the United States *after his reforms* will be similar to what are living here now. His proposal is similar to Texas Senator Kay Bailey Hutchison, who proposed a similar idea, in which illegal aliens go back to Mexico and then come back to stay.) American Enterprise Institute fellow Mark Thiessen explained this:

"This is a policy called "touchback" and it was first proposed in 2007 by moderate Republican Sen. Kay Bailey Hutchison (TX). She offered a "touchback" amendment on the Senate floor that would have required illegal immigrants to return to their home countries to apply for a special "Z visa" that would allow them to reenter the United States in an expedited fashion

and work here indefinitely…. Her amendment lost by a relatively close margin, 53-45. It was supported by most Republicans and even got five Democratic votes — Sens. Claire McCaskill, Max Baucus, Jon Tester, Byron Dorgan and John Rockefeller all voted for it."[125]

The idea was considered so reasonable that in an April 22, 2007, article in The New York Times *noted, "It's not ideal, but if a touch back provision is manageable and reassures people that illegal immigrants are indeed going to the back of the line, then it will be defensible." So Donald Trump is supporting an idea supported by the leftist* New York Times. *And as Marc Thiessen added, "In 2007,* The Los Angeles Times *did the first telephone poll of illegal immigrants* and asked whether they would go home under a *"touchback" law that allowed them to return with legal status. Sixty-three percent said yes, 27 percent said no and 10 percent were undecided. If they were promised a path to citizenship* when they returned, the number who said they would leave and return legally grew to 85 percent."[126] Trump's son, Eric, told Megyn Kelly, *"The point isn't just deporting them, it's deporting them and letting them back in legally. He's been so clear about that and I know the liberal media wants to misconstrue it, but its deporting them and letting them back legally."*[127]

Donald Trump added to this when he told CNN, *"I would get people out and then have an expedited way of getting them back into the country so they can be legal….A lot of these people are helping us…and sometimes it's jobs a citizen of the United States doesn't want to do. I want to move 'em out, and we're going to move 'em back in and let them be legal."*[128] Trump's own position on immigration may prove the beginning of a Republican compromise beginning with border security. Both Rubio and Cruz would agree with that compromise.

Fred Bauer on *National Review Online* noted about the immigration debate, *"Plenty of people who are much more serious about enforcing immigration law than Chuck Schumer also support legalization—but only after enforcement has been put in place. I don't know anyone who would call Mark Krikorian an open-borders fanatic, but he has supported legalization (and even a path to citizenship) for illegal immigrants. However, he has argued that enforcement should precede legalization. It would be bizarre in the extreme to say that Krikorian and Schumer basically have the same position on immigration because they both are open to a path to citizenship. When and under what conditions legalization happens is perhaps as important as whether it should happen at all."* [129]

Cato Institute policy analyst Alex Nowrasteh noted about Cruz, *"Senator Cruz's amendments support increasing skilled immigration, restricting welfare access to legalized immigrants who used to be unlawful, allowing for the legalization of unlawful immigrants but blocking their path to citizenship, guaranteeing that states can still check for proof of citizenship before allowing people to vote, and creating border security benchmarks that trigger the legalization program once they are met. His record on immigration is mixed, but he is far from a restrictionist."* [130] (In fairness, Cruz voted against the final bill.)

In the 2016 general election, Rubio in his Senate race not only outperformed Trump in Florida overall but even among minorities. He showed that reformist conservatism could be sold beyond the Republican base as he received 17 percent of black voters and 48 percent of Hispanic votes. Rubio received 62 percent of the Cuban voters and nearly 40 percent of non-Cuban voters; which made up nearly 63 percent of Republican Hispanic voters in Florida. While Trump received slightly more white voters compared to Rubio in his Senate re-election bid, 64 percent to 62 percent, Trump received about half of Rubio's votes among black voters and only received 35 percent as many Hispanic voter as Rubio did. While Trump received 54 percent of Cuban Hispanic voters, he received only 26 percent of non-Cuban voters, about 3 percent less than he received from Hispanic voters nationally.

Rubio not only did well among white voters but he also ran well among minorities, showing that the reform conservatism that he promoted during his presidential run and Senate race can attract Democrats. The debate on taxes and immigration showed while there were differences in approaches between Cruz and Rubio's beliefs, both senators had the same objective of expanding conservatism to include blue collar whites and minorities. It could be argued that Rubio is not much different in his tactics in appealing to voters as Trump. In Florida, Rubio's tactics ensured an election victory.

What Needs to Be Done

Americas PAC has been involved in every national election since 2003. (In 2002, many of the Americas PAC staff, led by the late Richard Nadler, operated as "Citizens for Better Government" before the formation of Americas PAC.) Many super PACS were formed in the wake of *Citizens United* but Americas PAC have been working to promote conservative ideas nearly a decade longer than most super PACS.

Americas PAC have run campaigns in 20 states and placed some 250,000 radio and TV ads, along with social media campaigns and newspaper campaigns. Many of the ads have been run on minority media outlets. Since 2012, Americas PAC have expanded into spreading the conservative message to Independents, blue collar and rural whites, as well as single white females along with other members of the Democratic base to expand the conservative majority. Americas PAC has succeeded in expanding the conservative base where others have failed. After the 2014 elections, Americas PAC and Americas Majority Foundation have polled 25,000 voters to gaining an idea of what worked in 2014 and what would work in 2016. Throughout the 2016 elections and after the election, Americas PAC and Americas Majority Foundation polled some 70,000 voters either nationally or in key battleground states.

Humans are very good at recognizing patterns, and they see that as the government grows, their opportunities for economic success shrink. National polls show that voters see an inverse correlation between government spending and their personal success. There is a new prevailing economic agreement: Government spending hurts the economy. Voters are rejecting Keynesian economics but neither party has yet to close the sale. Republicans are faring poorly because they aren't selling the product voters want to buy, thus allowing Donald Trump and his National Populism to attract significant numbers of the Republican electorate.

Business is about solving the customer's 'problem.' Every product or service sold—from the trivial to the lifesaving—solves a customer's problem. Republicans need to start viewing voters as customers, and doing in-depth consumer research to understand the problem they really want a solution to and the product voters will buy to solve that problem. To maintain their chances of winning the 2018 midterm elections and the 2020 presidential race, Republicans must understand the dynamics of voter's needs—including that the average voter does not trust the government to protect their interests. Americas Majority Foundation researcher JD Johannes noted, "The voters, as customers, want to buy a product that solves this *problem*. But the Democrats and Congressional Republicans are selling the same forty-year-old products."

Here is the good news. In our 2013 Illinois survey, respondents were given a generic Democratic plan which included increased spending for infrastructure, education, and job training while raising the minimum wage and taxing the rich compared to the Republican plan, which included keeping spending in line, reducing the deficits, stopping implementation of Obamacare, and keeping the tax rates the same. A year before the 2014 race, voters in blue Illinois barely supported the Democratic plan by a margin of 52 percent to 48 percent. When we simply stated the plans as the Obama plan and the Republican plan, 40 percent of Illinois voters supported the Obama plan and 37 percent supported the Republican plan, with the rest undecided.

In 2014, Republicans made a strong showing in Illinois when they took the governorship and two congressional seats and Sen. Dick Durbin was held to 53 percent of the vote against weak competition. We ran ads that argued that rising government spending and debt reduced voters' economic opportunities and these ads succeeded in persuading voters to vote for Republicans. Voters, our customers, knew that the Obama economic plan produced eight years of stagnation and that they no longer benefitted from Democratic policies. But the rise of Donald Trump shows that many Republicans don't even trust their own party to follow through on producing opportunities to succeed. So they nominated an outsider.

Democrats have been good at framing their ideas as a way to solve the customer's problem. The customer is no longer buying the Democratic plan, but they were still willing to buy their product in 2008 and 2012.

The number of Democrats voting for Hillary Clinton showed that millions are still willing to at least listen to Democrats. Republicans have the advantage that voters agree with them on the key issue of government spending's effect upon the economy. But the G.O.P has yet to find a way to sell their plan as a way to solve voters' problems. Trump's proposals will increase government debt and the deficit. He did not make any serious effort to address voters' concerns of reducing debt and deficits in the general election. What he promised to do was to "Make America Great Again." As Americas Majority Foundation associate J D Johannes noted, "Too often politicians and their consultants view voters as blocs or market segments. *For Democrats, this makes sense since they view voters as part of demographic groups but Republicans and conservatives succeed when they view voters not as blocs with specific issues, but address major macro concerns.*"

Voters see the big trend that as government debt and government spending has increased, their opportunities to move up the economic ladder have shrunk and their real income has dropped. Going into the 2016 election, voters viewed politicians, in particular Republicans, as the problem because they are not selling what voters want to buy: *A Fair Opportunity to Succeed.* Trump's success in the Republican primary showed he was selling voters that he can make America great again, which included a fair opportunity to succeed. Trump understood that voters wanted change, and he provided that.

Republicans needed to defend Senate seats in blue states, and as part of their defense, Republicans pointed out what the customer wants and needs. They contended that increased government spending and debt hurts the economy and a stronger economy creates a fair opportunity to succeed for everyone. Republicans and conservatives sold what the customer wants. They began to articulate a message that stopping out of control government spending and debt will provide the working and middle class with a chance to move up the economic ladder. The problem is that the political class and much of the mainstream media in the past framed the debate over deficits, pension obligations or debt ceiling as a solving of a *government* problem. The debate ends up as being how we need to preserve government at present spending levels or the need to spend even more to ensure the government stays solvent. Republicans need to treat this not as a government problem but as a *voter's* problem. If they hope to realign a new coalition capable of winning elections and governing effectively they need to show how they will reduce government and expand the private sector.

Democrats want to increase spending and are not concerned about creating more government debt as they move toward Democratic Socialism. Republicans must once again become the party of opportunity. J.D Johannes observed, "Republicans and conservatives have the opportunity to rebuild a new conservative majority and unite activist libertarians, social conservatives, pro-life advocates, gun rights advocates, and fiscal, small government conservatives with a broad swath of the general public under the prevailing economic agreement…A solid majority of Americans understand Keynesian economics has failed and government debt and spending are bad for the economy. It goes even further because the increased debt fuels the expansion of the bureaucratic state. The IRS is being used to silence political opposition, NSA spying scandals and the attack on gun rights are connected to ever-expanding government…*Social conservatives should be concerned about the ever-growing State encroaching on religious freedom by interfering with the religious sacrament of marriage and forcing religious institutions to violate their beliefs on the sanctity of life.*"

The original key to winning 2016 was for Republicans and conservatives to create an alliance that combines the concerns of different groups, including those who are concerned for gun rights, privacy rights, and those who fear the loss of religious freedom, in stopping expanding government while increasing economic freedom and economic opportunity. This coalition appeared threatened by Donald Trump's National Populism but as the 2016 election proceeded, Trump adopted many of the Republican Party's ideas about reforming government spending and tax policies that promoted growth and opportunity. The Republican candidates who articulated a message of ***A Fair Opportunity to Succeed*** put themselves in the best position to win whether on a presidential level, a state-wide level, or a congressional level. Among those who pushed that message in Senate races were Ron Johnson, whose business acumen gave him a leg up on making the argument on job creation since he actually created jobs as a businessman, and Marco Rubio, who built a broad coalition including near half of the Hispanic votes in Florida. Rod Blum succeeded in a Democratic district by running as a conservative reformer who can move his agenda. These candidates talked about economic opportunity and growth; and they got more votes than the head of the ticket, Donald Trump, did in their districts or states. .

Going into 2018, the message should still be the same: *a fair opportunity to succeed*. What voters want to see are solutions to their problems, beginning with stagnant income. However, past solutions may no longer be applicable today as many voters are not as affected by drops in marginal tax rates, but they are affected by a shrinking private sector compared to an ever-expanding federal government. In the past Republicans have talked about tax cuts, but it is time for a review of what supply side economics means in a nation with 20 trillion dollars in debts and where a half-billion-dollar deficit in a fiscal year is considered a minor miracle.

It is time to rediscover the supply side of economics and expand upon it. In the past, economic conservatives have concentrated on taxes but not on spending. The Heritage Foundation over the past two decades has rated countries by economic freedom. The foundation concluded that countries with the highest rating for overall economic freedom were often the most prosperous and equally important, most were politically free. The Heritage ratings didn't just include taxes but also national budgets, regulations, how easy it was to start a business, and how open these countries were to trade.

JD Johannes added, *"People have been hearing about tax cuts for a generation and it is not a motivating factor for most voters. I doubt voters see tax cuts as the solution to their problems. And in our current situation, more free capital sloshing around is not a guarantee of innovation that will drive value creation, higher wages and more jobs. Tax cuts are not bad...the voters just don't see them delivering what they want...Factories run on electricity and the US is in a position to have the cheapest, most reliable electricity in the world. Regulations that increase the cost of energy reduce our competitive position in manufacturing."* Supply siders have lost sight that an economic recovery is not just about taxes but removing those forces that inhibit economic growth that give an American worker chance at advancement.

It is time to realize that government spending is an important consideration of a prosperous society, and prosperity won't last long with massive government deficits or long-term federal debt that is nearly equal to the overall productive value of the nation. As America slipped in the Heritage Foundation ratings over the past fifteen years from being free to almost free, it is no coincidence that the average American had stagnant income growth and the nation as a whole had slow economic growth compared to other past recoveries. (In fairness, the decline in economic growth began during the George W. Bush and accelerated during the Obama years.)

Many argue that while Americans don't view increased government spending as a solution to their problems, they are not keen on seeing their favorite program cut. If the Trump administration just put a lid on overall spending and imposed a spending freeze while cutting taxes and regulations, the resulting growth would significantly reduce the deficit, if not put it in surplus.

Imagine if a President simply stated, "We will keep the budget the same for the next four years." There is a recent model to this as the Republicans called Obama's bluff in putting the sequester in place starting in 2011. The most significant budget deficit reduction during the Obama years occurred after the sequester was passed and while this did result in cuts in the Defense Department budget, a spending freeze doesn't mean you can't set priorities. One way to begin the process of spending reduction is simply review our different departments and ask about each one, "Can we live without it?" One place to start is the Department of Energy which the fracking revolution has made obsolete. If you eliminate departments, you eliminate the need to spend in a particular area and you can send government funds to areas where the needs are greater.

In 2010, President Obama's own budget commission recommended a combination of budget cutting, tax reforms including lower marginal tax rates and closing loopholes. So there were Democrats willing to listen to reasonable ideas and there were bipartisan solutions that could gain traction. (The commission's overall tax plans would have increased taxes on most Americans but the commission accepted the need to lower marginal tax rates as well as the need to increase overall wealth. The commission also supported other tax reform plans that were revenue neutral.)

Regulation is another area to discover the supply side and this is one area that Trump has gotten it right with his plan to eliminate older regulations when new ones are created. The regulations imposed by Dodd-Frank have benefited the bigger banks and financial institutions since they have the capital to deal with the increased regulations compared to smaller and medium size banks. Since Dodd-Frank, bigger banks have gained market share at the expense of smaller ones, the very banks that serve much of

Main Street. This simply shows that regulations do hurt the middle class and the institutions they depend upon. The EPA's war on coal has made it more difficult for coal to compete with natural gas and has cost the coal industry many high paying jobs. So supply siders needs to concentrate not just on reducing taxes but understanding that reducing spending and regulations will also have the supply side effect of increasing growth.

There are Democratic strategists who understand this dynamic, but their Achilles heel is that they are so concerned with what individuals make or don't make that they forget that a growing private sector provides opportunity for all. As John F. Kennedy remarked a half-century ago, "A rising tide lifts all boats."

Crime and Safety

Sunset Park in Brooklyn is a predominately Hispanic community and over the past few years, whites have begun to move in as they look for less expensive place to live outside of Park Slope or Manhattan. The process of gentrification has begun. In the early 1990s my youngest daughter told me that Sunset Park was dominated by gang wars but today it is as safe as downtown Cedar Rapids or Marion, Iowa, where I live. At night, restaurants are full, small convenience stores, bakery, and grocery stores are busy, and there is a taco stand at the corner of 38th Street and 5th Avenue operating at night. The crime rate has significantly dropped from the early 1990s. I told my daughter, "This is the legacy of Rudy Giuliani." New York is probably the safest major metropolitan area and so far, not even leftist mayor Bill DeBasio has reversed this positive trend with his anti-police mentality.

During the 2016 election, law and order became an issue and while the crime rate is significantly lower than the early 1990s, voters view crime as an issue. The reason would include the increased numbers of police officers killed in the line of duty and the publicity surrounding the murder rate of major cities such as Chicago. Over the past year, homicides shot up 12 percent nationwide. In cities of between 500,000 and a million people there has been a 14.5 percent rise in murders. In cities of a million or more, this increase has reached 20 percent.

The Pew Research Center notes that 57 percent of voters—and 78 percent of Trump supporters—see crime as increasing since 2008. Violent crimes have fallen by 19 percent since 2008 and property crime has fallen 23 percent during this period, the average voter sees 2015 as that year that something changed as crime did increase that one year. Even Hillary Clinton supporters, by a margin of 37 percent to 25 percent view the crime rate as increasing.[131]

A Gallup poll in October 2016 found that 60 percent of voters thought the problem of crime was "extremely" or "very" serious. While these numbers were unchanged from 2015, Gallup found that voters' concerns in the past two years was the highest in this century. Seventy percent of voters thought the crime rate had increased. By a margin of 45 percent to 33 percent, voters viewed crime increasing in their area.[132]

What voters may be viewing is a change in attitude toward crime. Since the incident in Ferguson, Missouri, and the rise of Black Lives Matter, many voters have seen policing changing in major ways. Manhattan Institute Heather Mac Donald stated, *"Staring in the second half 2014 however, after the shooting of Michael Brown and Ferguson, Missouri…crime in heavily black neighborhoods starting going up because again officers are backing off of policing under the relentless hostility they get on the streets and under the message that they are the biggest threat facing young black men."* [133]

Many in the public see this and wonder if we are seeing a national trend of police officers easing up on aggressive tactics that helped reduce crime in the first place. The crime rate is nowhere near what we saw two decades ago before Congress passed new laws that increased incarceration for violent and repeat offenders as part of "get tough on crime" laws enacted during the Clinton administration. NBC News noted in a online article, *"The Violent Crime Control and Law Enforcement Act of 1994 contained an expansion of the federal death penalty to include drug offenses, the "Three Strikes, You're Out" rule, and billions in funding for police, prisons, and states that made it harder for people to get parole (though Mr. Clinton neglected to mention this when he mentioned that most prisoners are incarcerated by the state)…But if Bill and Hillary Clinton were the pot, black politicians, activists, and pastors were the kettle. Their support of punitive measures actually paved the way for Clinton."* [134] The majority of the Congressional Black Caucus, led by Rep. Kweisi Mfume (D—Maryland), supported the bill as a way to rid their communities of gang violence. In the 1990s, violent crimes such as rapes, assaults, and murders were at record highs in the inner cities.

The bipartisan consensus that existed in the 1990s to fight crime no longer exists. Many black activists and legislators view the war on crime as responsible for the increased incarceration of blacks. As LA Batchelor of the radio show *Batchelor Pad* mentioned to me on a debate of stop and frisk tactics, *"It is the blacks who get frisked, not the whites."*

The dilemma for many blacks is this: while their history with law enforcement has led to distrusting the police, will this distrust lead to increased crime in their neighborhood? Blacks are the most likely to be victims of crime, but many blacks do not view the police as their protectors or friends and do not see the police as on their side. They don't trust the people whose job it is to defend them. As we see in polls on gun rights, blacks are supportive of the right to defend themselves, but until trust is built between police and the community, the risk of crime returning to 1990s levels exist. A community can't be prosperous without being safe to live in.

Many voters are seeing their government backing away from protecting them and thus the polls are reflecting not so much of what is happening today but the fear of what will happen tomorrow. In spite of the rise in crime from 2014 to 2015, the overall crime rate is down from 2008 but voters' fear of the future is what driving the poll numbers. Going into 2018 and 2020, law and order may be the sleeper issue since voters understand that safety ensures prosperity in their community. The issue of economics and being safe from crime are intertwined and in the voters mind, the political class is not interested in doing the steps to protect them. Just as many voters supported Trump over border security, they also moved toward him in 2016 due to their belief that Trump cared for their safety. Trump himself in his acceptance speech stated, *"There can be no prosperity without law and order…Our convention occurs at a moment of crisis for our nation… The attacks on our police, and the terrorism in our cities, threaten our very way of life. Any politician who does not grasp this danger is not fit to lead our country…The first task for our new administration will be to liberate our citizens from the crime and terrorism and lawlessness that threatens their communities…The most basic duty of government is to defend the lives of its own citizens. Any government that fails to do so is a government unworthy to lead."* [135] Trump made the connection of prosperity and security within a community and many voters responded.

The peaceful community of Sunset Park is a reminder of what local government can do to secure a community and allow it to grow. If a government forgets the lessons that allowed communities to become free of crime, the law of the jungle will soon replace the rule of law designed to protect that community.

Conclusion

If you had asked me in October 2016, going into the final month of the presidential campaign, I would have stated that while Trump could win, he was the weakest Republican candidate and any other candidate would be up by double digit. Today, I would not be certain that any Republican would have beaten Hillary Clinton and maybe the only candidate who would have won this election was Donald Trump. Like many political operatives, I believed in the idea that only Hillary Clinton could lose to Trump and the only Republican who could have lost to Hillary Clinton was Trump. This was based on polls showing Trump running behind other Republican—particularly Rubio and Kasich—in a one-on-one campaign during the primary season before Trump officially wrapped it up.

Trump's higher negatives added to the idea that he was the weakest candidate. In a recent piece on whether any Republicans could have beaten Hillary, Michael Barone stated, *"Springtime polls seemed to assume the electorate would look much like the one in 2012. The signs that Trump would run much better than Romney among non-college-educated whites weren't very clear, particularly when his controversial comments caused his overall numbers to sag. Going well into the fall, few polls showed the surge of votes that decided the election in what I have called the outstate Midwest—the counties outside metropolitan areas with a million-plus people in Wisconsin, Michigan, Ohio and (sort-of-Midwestern) Pennsylvania, states with 64 electoral votes that went to Barack Obama in 2012 and Trump in 2016."* [136]

Barone's own view is that maybe this is not the case and I am now coming to the conclusion that it is not certain that any Republican could have won against Hillary Clinton. Barone noted, *"Iowa and the outstates, Trump won percentages higher than George W. Bush did in 2004, while Clinton ran far behind Obama's 2012 showing — 12 points behind in outstate*

Ohio, 11 points behind in Iowa and outstate Michigan, 9 points behind in outstate Wisconsin and 8 points behind in outstate Pennsylvania. These are all places with many non-college-educated whites and few blacks, Hispanics, and Asians. Trump's stands on trade and immigration — distinctly different from those of other Republicans—were surely partly responsible for his out-state margins, and it seems unlikely another Republican nominee could have matched them.[137]

These interpretations are all theoretical. But the Florida results, where we saw Marco Rubio defeat Pat Murphy and Donald Trump won the state Electoral College votes, provide important additional evidence. While this is an apple to orange comparison, and Rubio ran ahead of Trump, there are some interesting data in the state exit polls.

As the Florida exit polls showed, Rubio had 62 percent among white voters, including 63 percent among white males, 62 percent white females, 62 percent of white college graduates, and 62 percent of white non-college graduates, while Trump had 64 percent of the white voters including 67 percent of the white males, 60 percent of the white females, 62 percent of white college graduates, and 66 percent of white non-college graduates. Both Rubio and Trump did well among whites, but Rubio ran two percentage points behind Trump among white voters and ran four percent behind white non-college graduates.

Rubio had 48 percent of Hispanic voters, compared to Trump's 35 percent overall percentage among Hispanics. Both candidates did well among Cubans, with Rubio grabbing 68 percent of the Cuban Hispanic voters while Trump had 54 percent of Cuban voters. Among non-Cuban Hispanics, Rubio garnered 39 percent and Trump had 26 percent. Rubio slightly doubled Trump support among black voters by 17 percent to 8 percent.[138]

Rubio had broader support in Florida than Donald Trump did nationally. But the American election system it is about winning specific states. One has to ask if a Rubio coalition been enough to take battleground states just as Pennsylvania, Michigan, and Wisconsin. Rubio may have carried more black voters than Trump, but would he have lost ground among white voters in these key Midwestern states? Rubio's 48 percent share of the Hispanic voters is inflated due to the impact of Cuban voters and 39 percent among non-Cuban voters would be a more realistic number. These numbers might have been enough to carry Nevada and Colorado but if Rubio ran some couple of percentage points behind Trump among white voters in these Midwest states, he would most likely have lost those states.

FiveThirtyEight's Harry Enten reviewed Joni Ernst's victory over Bruce Braley in a 2014 Iowa Senate race. He found that white voters without college degrees shifted toward Ernst, ensuring her victory by 8.5 percent where pollsters predicted she would win by 1.5 percent. As Enten predicted, *"If that shift persists, it could have a big effect on the Presidential race in 2016, altering the White House math by eliminating the Democratic edge in the Electoral College."* [139]

Real Clear Politics's Sean Trende foresaw Trump's strategy when he wrote in 2013, *"But the GOP still has something of a choice to make. One option is to go after these downscale whites…it can probably build a fairly strong coalition this way. Doing so would likely mean nominating a candidate who is more Bush-like in personality, and to some degree on policy. This doesn't mean embracing "big government" economics or redistribution full bore; suspicion of government is a strain in American populism dating back at least to Andrew Jackson. It means abandoning some of its more pro-corporate stances. This GOP would have to be more "America first" on trade, immigration and foreign policy; less pro-Wall Street and big business in its rhetoric; more Main Street/populist on economics…For now, the GOP seems to be taking a different route, trying to appeal to Hispanics through immigration reform and to upscale whites by relaxing its stance on some social issues. I think this is a tricky road to travel, and the GOP has rarely been successful at the national level with this approach. It certainly has to do more than Mitt Romney did, who at times seemed to think that he could win the election just by corralling the small business vote. That said, with the right candidate it could be doable. It's certainly the route that most pundits and journalists are encouraging the GOP to travel, although that might tell us more about the socioeconomic standing and background of pundits and journalists than anything else…Of course, the most successful Republican politicians have been those who can thread a needle between these stances: Richard Nixon, Ronald Reagan and (to a lesser degree) Bush 43 have all been able to talk about conservative economic stances without horrifying downscale voters. These politicians are rarities, however, and the GOP will most likely have to make a choice the next few cycles about which road it wants to travel."* [140]

As shown in this book, Trump understood what his rivals failed to see, that the Democrats viewed that white blue-collar voters were locked into their party or that the new coalitions of minorities, Millennials, city dwellers, and members of public sector unions formed the basis of a new majority. However this coalition was checked by Trump's ability to attract many blue-collar workers. Hillary Clinton failed to capture Obama's share of the minority votes and this cost her in many of the battleground states. As Michael Barone noted, *"Now we have a more downscale Republican party and a Democratic party confined to its coastal and campus cocoons. We'll see how that works out."* [141]

I began this book discussing the rise of National Populism and Democratic Socialism. National Populism is not a body of policies but a reaction from the disappointments of the past century in which many have seen little rise in their incomes and opportunities and their values mocked. The biggest fear for conservatives is that National Populism will encourage the rise of a second big government party as populists view government intervention as a solution for the problems of the middle class by promoting economic growth. The principle that government is the creator of wealth is what drives Democratic Socialism. Many within National Populism also find this principle appealing.

As for the alt-right, it is neither conservative nor right wing but just another version of Marxist or fascist thought. The difference between the alt-right and many other Marxists is its orientation toward white racial identity, but its disdain toward free markets or the rule of law is not much different from their fellow Marxists. The alt right is a small minority but the bigger problem is not the rise of the alt-right, but attempting to redefine the alt-right as part of a broader Populist movement while downplaying the alt-right's fascist and racist ideology. Donald J. Trump in a post-election *New York Times* interview repudiated the alt-right movement. Conservatives and National Populists should follow Trump's lead and disavow the movement its racism and white supremacy. Trump's supporters are not racists, and there are many areas where many National Populists and reform conservatives agree, including tax and immigration reforms that begin with border security. The duty of reform conservatives will be to remind the National Populists that wealth doesn't begin with government but the individual.

The greater threat to our freedom comes from the Democratic Socialist movement. While a reform conservative movement can counter National Populists, there are no counterpoints to the Democratic Socialist movement since many moderates have either been defeated in elections or have simply left the Democratic Party. The Democratic donor class funds the socialist movement with glee and the Democratic Party has become the party of the rich and the poor. As the Democratic Party has shown over the past eight years, they have no problem in using government to attack their opponents as we detailed in this book including the use of the IRS to target conservative political organization. The left likes to portray Trump as the second coming of Hitler or Mussolini, but while one may question Trump's view of the media and the First Amendment, it has been the Democratic Party which is a real threat to many of our freedoms, beginning with free speech and free political association.

After 2014, we concluded, *"Republicans and conservatives need to start selling a product the customer wants to buy and articulate a common message theme that stopping the out of control government debt is the way to fix the economy, to create jobs and provide the working and middle class with a fair opportunity to success, but the Democrats just want to create more government debt...View it in this way, Telecommunications is a market segment. But consumers don't buy telecommunications, they buy an iPhone or an Android phone. Improving the economy is an issue segment, a market segment. Consumers really want to buy a result, a specific product, the opportunity to succeed...A solid majority of Americans understand Keynesian economics has failed and government debt and spending are bad for the economy. It goes even further because the increased debt fuels the expansion of the bureaucratic state. The IRS being used to silence political opposition, the NSA spying scandals and the attack on gun rights are connected to ever expanding government...Many other issues like life, marriage and the Second Amendment, though seen as less important by most customers, should not be ignored, but framed in the context of the growing power and scope of the state...Social conservatives should be concerned about the ever-growing state encroaching on religious freedom by interfering with the religious sacrament of marriage and forcing religious institutions to violate their beliefs on the sanctity of life... Republican candidates who articulate a message of creating A Fair Opportunity to Succeed by stopping the out of control government debt and spending that hurts the economy will be selling a product the customer actually wants to buy.*" [142]

What Trump did was to unite myriad factions behind a one single theme: Make America Great Again. Trump theme's for the middle class was simple: he would give them a *Fair Opportunity to Succeed* by reforming their taxes, bring jobs home, and creating new jobs while securing the border. He set a tone that it was reasonable to love our country and its institutions. For many social conservatives and gun rights advocates, their battleground was the Supreme Court, where they hoped to persuade the Court to preserve their rights to religious freedom and the right to defend themselves. Approximately four million more evangelical Christians voted than Hispanics and blacks combined, and Trump received 80 percent of those evangelical votes.

The lessons of the 2016 election began with the theme that we saw in 2014. The average voter understands that the old way of doing things have failed and it is time for a new direction. They reject Keynesian economic policies of spending ever more money and gaining ever more debt; our polls have shown that for past three years. The Republicans are now the party of Main Street and the Party of Middle America while the Democrats are depending upon conclaves in major cities and the coast to maintain their power. Without California, where the Republican Party has ceased to exist as a statewide entity, Hillary Clinton wouldn't even won the popular vote. Her entire margin was in one state and without that state, she would have even lost the popular vote. California is the Democratic future for America, a state where the widest income disparity exists, where the very rich have sealed itself from the very poor while the entrepreneurs and the middle class have moved out. California is a state rich in resources and a state government refusing to allow the maximum use of their resources.

Joel Kotkin, a Democrat, has been in the forefront of detailing the struggle of the middle class and has been outspoken about his own party's role in increasing the divide between rich and poor. Many of his ideas actually would appeal more to Republicans and Independents than his own party and he has been critical of what he calls the "left oligarchies," like Mark Zuckerberg and the rest of Silicon Valley, who have rigged the system in their favor. Kotkin recently noted a conversation with a young Republican senator that the biggest conflict within the Republican Party is between the donor class and the grassroots Republicans. I sometime view this as a little too simple, since the GOP donor class is as divided on many issues. The Koch brothers differ from Paul Singer on foreign affairs; and Foster Friess, a major donor, is a supporter of conservatives on social issues and has been sympathetic to blue collar Republicans, whereas other major donors are more liberal on social issues.

There are similarities between the donor class, and one area is tax policies as they are looking for growth-oriented policies. But for many in the middle class, they are less interested in tax cuts than more broad-based policies that will increase their own income. They are not as enthusiastic about lower tax rates for the wealthy as Republican donors are.

The majority of Trump supporters are working class and middle class. They are the forgotten Americans. Many of these middle-class voters may have been Reagan Democrats, and these voters are concerned about immigration since many of them view increased immigration as a threat to their own path to success.

Joel Kotkin added, *"Immigration, for many of them, is also an economic issue, as it creates more competition for jobs and, in some cases, as we have seen recently with the H-1B visa program, has been shamelessly used by companies to separate even educated Americans from their jobs…Nor is Silicon Valley, still heroic in the minds of some conservatives, necessarily seen as a boon by these Republicans. As left-leaning journalist Steven Hill has pointed out, the 'share economy,' promoted by the likes of Uber and Airbnb, also 'disrupts' the pattern of full-time employment once enjoyed by millions of Americans. These firms may proffer a 'techno-utopian future,' dominated by these 'disruptive' businesses, and enjoy strong ties to the Obama Democratic Party, but they are turning many workers into what Hill calls 'tumbleweeds adrift in the labor market.'"* [143]

Trump has many failings including making a fortune as a crony capitalist making his own deals with government regulators and Democratic politicians, but part of his appeal lies with his own view of the political class which he is forever calling "stupid." He understands that much of America no longer trusts government, but this distrust goes to other institutions of the ruling class, including corporations and Wall Street. Trump is appealing to Independents and working-class Democrats who know the old rules of the game no longer work for them, ensuring and they are alienated from politics. As Joel Kotkin noted, *"One has to go back to Reagan to find a Republican Party that could consistently position itself as populist. Reagan's appeal was based on security and taxes; for today's GOP, the issue should be – besides terrorism and rising crime – how to address the decline of the middle- and working-class economy."* [144] In the past, Democrats appealed to the middle class with programs designed for the middle class including the G.I. Bill and had no problem with fighting class warfare. Hillary Clinton's campaign attempted to appeal to the middle class through welfare expansion geared strictly to them but Hillary, like Obama, is building a Democratic base based less than on class and more on race and identity politics. Many of this new left-wing coalition is built around Millennials, minorities, singles, and academics as well as wealthy tech executives. However, Obama's rejection of the Keystone pipeline and his war on fossil fuels was a dagger aimed at many blue-collar Democrats. With coal mines closing due to EPA regulations, many blue-collar voters who voted for Bill Clinton in 1992 were abandoned by his wife and her party in 2016.

Our data showed consistently that average Americans agree that Keynesian economics no longer works for them as increased debt and deficits are ruining their fair chance to succeed. They prefer economic growth and job creation to dealing with inequality and even saving the planet by dealing with climate change. They don't care what the planet's temperature is if they are being asked to live in a society where they cannot advance.

For four decades, the Republicans have depended upon a coalition of social conservatives, national security hawks and supply siders. But this coalition that elected Reagan is now fraying and is no longer the majority. The good news is that the left has abandoned the blue collar white voters as well as many within their minority base who have more in common with these white blue collars than with other parts of the Democratic base. These minorities own their businesses and are moving into the middle class, but they are seeing their own doors being shut by the oligarchies that fund the Democratic left. The door is open for Republicans and reformist conservatives who understand that Republican Party is now the Party of Main Street. It is time for Wall Street to understand their long-term health is dependent upon a healthy Main Street. Wall Street can't survive in the long run if nothing is produced on Main Street.

The Republicans now have the opportunity to rebuild a new Conservative Majority, based on conservative ideals beginning with this: *the average American wants and needs a Fair Opportunity to Succeed.*

Acknowledgments

I want to thank my associate, JD Johannes, for his help, research and advice during this project and thanks to Katharine Donelson, soon to be Doctor Katharine Donelson for her own advice, and finally, Martin Morse Wooster for his help in editing the final book. I would love to thank Janice, my wife for her patience while I was concentrating on the book.

About the Author

Tom Donelson has been involved in politics for four decades, run campaigns in over 20 states, and presently chairs Americas PAC and is the Project Director/research associate at Americas Majority Foundation.

Endnotes

Chapter One

1. Andrew Hartman, *A War for the Soul of America: A History of the Culture Wars* (Chicago: University of Chicago Press, 2015), 3.
2. Charles Murray, "Trump's America," *Wall Street Journal*, February 12, 2016.
3. Ibid.
4. Michael Wolff, "Ringside With Steve Bannon at Trump Tower as the President-Elect's Strategist Plots 'An Entirely New Political Movement,'" *The Hollywood Reporter*, November 18, 2016.
5. Joan Hoff Wilson, *Herbert Hoover: Forgotten Progressive* (Boston: Little, Brown, 1965). 68.
6. Steve Horwitz, "Herbert Hoover: Father of the New Deal," Cato Institute, 2011.
7. Marc A. Thiessen, "Message For the G.O.P.: Trump Supports Amnesty," American Enterprise Institute, November 23, 2015.
8. Byron York, "A Brief History of Trump's Outrageousness," *Washington Examiner*, November 23, 2015.
9. Jeremy Diamond, "Trump's Immigration Plan: Deport the Undocumented, 'Legal Status' For Some," CNN.com, July 30, 2015.
10. "Bernie Sanders Meets With the Daily News Editorial Board," *New York Daily News*, April 1, 2016.
11. Eric Liu and Nick Hanauer, "The True Origins of Prosperity," *Democracy*, Summer 2013.
12. Ibid.
13. John Harwood, "10 Questions for Bernie Sanders," cnbc.com, May 26, 2015.

14 John Hinderaker, "The Obama Administration's Idea of a Crime…" Power Line, March 10, 2016.

15 Ibid.

16 Jeff Tollefson, "Global Warming 'Hiatus' Debate Flares Up Again," *Nature*, February 24, 2016.

17 John Hinderaker, "The Great Free Speech Issue of Our Time," Power Line, March 3, 2016.

18 Ben Boychuk, "State to Climate Change Skeptics: Shut Up, Already," *Sacramento Bee,* July 9, 2016.

19 Maxim Lott, "Climate Spin: Behind-The-Scenes Emails Show Profs Evading Questions," Fox News, June 1, 2016.

20 John Hinderaker, "The Latest Scott Walker Smear, Debunked," *Power Line*, June 19, 2014.

21 Jesse Richman and David Earnest, "Could Non-Citizens Decide the November Election?" washingtonpost.com, October 24, 2014 (italics added).

22 "Not Rigged, Thrown: Bill Campenni Comments," Power Line, October 20, 2016.

23 J. Christian Adams, "Podesta WikiLeaks Horror: Voter ID Doesn't Stop Alien Voting," PJ Media, October 21, 2016.

24 Another factor that can't be discounted in North Carolina is that Libertarian candidate had slightly more than 2 percent of the vote and was another factor for McCrory's loss.

25 Jonathan Turley, "The Rise of the Fourth Branch of Government," *Washington Post*, May 24, 2013.

26 Ibid.

27 Ibid.

28 Ibid.

29 Ibid.

30 Ibid.

31 Allum Bokhari and Milo Yiannapoulos, "An Establishment Conservative's Guide to the Alt-Right," *Breitbart,* March 29, 2016 (Italics in text).

32 James Kirchick, "Among the Thugs," *National Review*, April 11, 2016.

33 Dota, "National Capitalism-A Third Alternative," *Alternative Right*, July 24, 2015.

34 Jonathan Turley and Sen. Ron Johnson, "Restoring Balance Among the Branches of Government in Washington," *Washington Post,* July 28, 2014.

35 Jonathan Swan, "Trump Advisors Tell the Republicans: You're No Longer Reagan Party," *The Hill,* November 23, 2016.

Chapter Two

36 Matt Latimer, "Joe Biden's 'Chains' Comment and the Racial Double Standard," The Daily Beast, August 15, 2012.

37 The 2016 Committee was a Super PAC designed to support Dr. Ben Carson, and then supported Donald J. Trump after Carson dropped out. It is now called the Stars and Stripes PAC. For information about the committee, see Joe Nahra, "The 2016 Committee," factcheck.org, February 3, 2016.

Chapter Three

38 LIBRE Initiative, "Survey of Voter Attitudes," March 2012.

39 McLaughlin and Associates, "YG Network: National Survey Results," May 2013.

40 Jim Norman, "Public Remains Wary of Federal Government's Power," Gallup, October 9, 2015.

41 "52 percent Say Government Won't Do Enough For Economy, 62 percent Want Cuts," Rasmussen Reports, October 24, 2013.

42 William A. Galston, "A Better Campaign Theme Than Inequality," *Wall Street Journal,* April 21, 2015.

43 "53 percent Rate Economic Growth as More Important Than Economic Fairness," Rasmussen Reports, January 14, 2014.

44 Global Strategy Group, "Focus on Growth to Frame Priorities," April 2014.

45 John Judis, "Dear Democrats: Populism Will Not Save You," *National Journal,* June 19, 2015.

46 Pew Research Center, *Trends in American Values, 1987-2012* (Washington: Pew Research Center, 2012),

47 Michael Barone, "Tyler Cowen's Future Shock: No More Average People," *Washington Examiner,* October 6, 2013.

48 "Bryan's 'Cross of Gold' Speech: Mesmerizing the Masses," History Matters website, historymatters.gmu.edu.

49 Judy Shelton, "Trump's Contribution to Sound Money," *Wall Street Journal*, August 10, 2016.

50 John McCormack and Terrence Dopp, "Free-Trade Opposition Unites Political Parties in National Poll," Bloomberg, March 24, 2016.

51 "Americans See Free Trade as Good For Business, Or Do They?" Rasmussen Reports, April 21, 2015.

52 John McCormack and Terrence Dopp, "Free Trade Opposition Unites Parties in National Poll."

53 Pew Research Center, "Campaign Exposes Fissures Over Issues, Values, and How Life Has Changed in the U.S.," March 31, 2016.

54 Justin McCarthy, "Americans Remain Upbeat About Foreign Trade," Gallup, February 16, 2016.

55 Art Swift, "In U.S, Record-High 72 percent See Foreign Trade As Opportunity," Gallup, February 16, 2017.

56 During a debate on the "Larry King Show" when NAFTA was being passed, Al Gore said that Rush Limbaugh was one of his sources defending free trade, possibly the only time Gore or any other Democrat would say that about Rush Limbaugh.

57 Mark Murray, "Majority of Voters Support Free Trade, Immigration: Poll," NBC News, July 17, 2016.

58 Frank Newport, "American Public Opinion on Foreign Trade," Gallup, April 1, 2016.

59 Adriano Pantoja, "Latino Voters Favor Gun Restrictions," Latino Decisions, March 12, 2013.

60 Emily Ekins, "Stricter Gun Control Laws Won't Prevent Criminals From Getting Guns, Say 63percent of Americans," reason.com, December 12, 2013.

61 Art Swift, "Personal Safety Top Reason Americans Own Guns Today," Gallup, October 28, 2013.

62 Jeffrey M. Jones, "Americans In Agreement With Supreme Court on Gun Rights," Gallup, June 26, 2008.

63 Tom Donelson and Adam Schaefer, "Winning the Hispanic Vote With Conservative Ideas," usnews.com, April 24, 2013.

[64] Mark Hugo-Lopez, Ana Gonzalez-Barrera and Jens Michael Krogstad, "Latino Support for Democrats Falls, But Democrats' Advantage Remains," Pew Research Center, October 29, 2014.

[65] "Romney 49 percent, Obama 48 percent in Gallup's Final Election Survey," Gallup, November 5, 2012.

[66] William Saletan, "We Won The White Vote," Slate, November 30, 2012.

[67] Andrew Dugan, "Married Voters Strongly Back Romney," Gallup, September 14, 2012.

[68] Suzanne Goldenberg, "Single Women Voted Overwhelmingly for Obama, Researchers Find," *Guardian*, November 9, 2012.

[69] Robert Rector, "Marriage: America's Greatest Weapon Against Child Poverty," Heritage Foundation, September 16, 2010.

[70] Robert Rector, "Married Fathers: America's Greatest Weapon Against Child Poverty," Heritage Foundation, June 16, 2010.

[71] Kay S. Hymowitz, "American Caste," *City Journal*, Spring 2012.

[72] Clare Malone, "Hillary Couldn't Win Over White Women," Fivethirtyeight.com, November 9, 2012.

[73] Alec Tyson and Shiv Maniam, "Behind Trump's Victory: Divisions By Race, Gender, Education," Pew Research Center, November 9, 2016.

[74] Sean Trende, *The Lost Majority: Why The Future of Government Is Up For Grabs—And Who Will Take It* (New York: Palgrave Macmillan, 2012), 163.

[75] Ibid.

[76] Scott Keeter, Juliana Horowitz, and Alec Tyson, "Young Voters In the 2008 Election." Pew Research Center, November 13, 2008.

[77] Ruy Teixeira and John Halpin, "The Path to 270: Demographics Versus Economics in the 2012 Presidential Election," Center for American Progress, November 2011.

[78] "Young Voters in the 2010 Election," Center for Information and Research on Civic Learning and Engagement, Tufts University, November 9, 2010.

[79] Emily Richmond, Mikhail Zinshteyn, and Natalie Gross, "Dissecting the Youth Vote," theatlantic.com, November 11, 2016.

Chapter Four

[80] For a summary of their book, see James C. Bennett and Michael J. Lotus, "America 3.0: The Coming Revolution of America," American Enterprise Institute, August 20, 2013.

81 Ramesh Ponnuru, "The Empire of Freedom," *National Review*, March 24, 2003.

82 Ibid.

83 James C. Bennett, "Our Emerging Anglosphere," *Orbis*, Winter 2002.

84 James C. Bennett, *The Anglosphere Challenge: Why The English-Speaking Nations Will Lead The Way in The Twenty-First Century* (Lanham, Maryland: Rowman and Littlefield, 2007)

85 Ibid, 80.

86 Ponnuru, "Empire of Freedom."

87 Ibid.

88 Bennett, *The Anglosphere Challenge*, 26.

89 Ibid, 27.

90 Ibid, 34.

91 Ibid, 35.

92 Ibid, 38.

93 Ibid, 287.

94 Pramit Pal Chaudhuri, "Indo-Russian Ties Going Nowhere," *Hindustan Times*, October 13, 2003.

95 James M. Gavin, *War and Peace in the Space Age* (New York: Harper, 1958), 64.

96 Thomas C. Reed, *At the Abyss: An Insider's History of the Cold War* (New York: Presidio/Ballantine, 2004), 347-48.

97 "Israeli Military Amazed, 'Jealous' At U.S. War Against Iraq," worldtribune.com, April 14, 2003.

98 Fred Kaplan, "Force Majeure," Slate, April 10, 2003.

99 Ibid.

100 "Conference de Press de Charles de Gaulle (14 janvier 1963)" in Charles de Gaulle, *Discours et Messages. Volume IV: Pour l'effort (1962-1965)*. Paris: Plon, 1970, 66-71

101 Bennett, *The Anglosphere Challenge*. 164.

102 Ibid, 167.

103 Ibid, 7.

104 Gurcharan Das, *India Unbound* (New York: Knopf, 2001), 83.

105 Henry Kissinger, *Does America Need a Foreign Policy? Toward a Diplomacy of the 21st Century* (New York: Simon and Schuster, 2001), 156.

106 Ibid,158.

107 Henry A. Kissinger, "India and Pakistan: After the Explosions," *Washington Post*, June 9, 1998.

108 Michael Barone, "What's Trump's Take on Foreign Policy?", syndicated column appearing December 16, 2016.

109 Niall Ferguson, "Donald Trump's New World Order," *The American Interest*, November 21, 2016.

110 Michael Barone, "What's Trump's Take on U.S. Foreign Policy?"

111 Ibid.

112 Ibid.

113 Niall Ferguson, "Donald Trump's New World Order."

114 Ibid.

115 Theodore Roosevelt, "First Annual Message to Congress, December 3, 1901," found on The American Presidency Project, presidency.ucsb.edu.

116 Niall Ferguson, "Donald Trump's New World Order."

117 Anne Bayefsky, "Diplomatic Terrorism at The UN, Courtesy President Obama," Fox News, December 24, 2016.

118 Mark P. Mills, "3 Myths About Our Natural Gas Boom," *USA Today*, April 3, 2014.

119 Ibid.

120 Albert Gallatin, *Memorial of the Committee Appointed by the 'Free Trade Convention,' Held at Philadelphia in September and October 1831, To Prepare and Present a Memorial To Congress Remonstrating Against the Existing Tariff of Duties* (New York: Wm. A. Mercein, 1832), 6.

121 Thomas Sowell, *Basic Economics: A Common Sense Guide to the Economy*, fourth edition (New York: Basic Books, 2011), 514.

122 Ibid, 513-14.

123 Michael Wolff, "Ringside at Trump Tower as the President-Elect's Strategist Plots 'An Entirely New Political Movement,'" *Hollywood Reporter*, November 18, 2016.

124 Jay Cost, *A Republic No More: Big Government and the Rise of Political Corruption* (New York: Encounter Books, 2015)

Chapter Five
125 Marc Thiessen, "Who Knew? Trump Favors Amnesty for Undocumented Immigrants," *Newsweek,* November 17, 2015.

126 Ibid.

127 Ibid.

128 Ibid.

129 Fred Bauer, "The Immigration Debate: Widening the Scope," National Review Online, December 17, 2015.

130 Alex Nowrasteh "Ted Cruz's Mixed Record on Immigration Reform," Cato Institute, November 13, 2015.

131 John Gramlich, "Voters' Perceptions of Crime Continue to Conflict With Reality," Pew Research Center, November 16, 2016.

132 Art Swift, "America's Perceptions of U.S. Crime Problem Are Steady." Gallup, November 9, 2016.

133 "Heather Mac Donald on Discretionary Policing, Violent Crime, and Black Lives Matter," The Federalist, June 21, 2016.

134 Yolanda Young: "Analysis: Black Leaders Supported Clinton's Crime Bill," NBC News, April 8, 2016.

135 Associated Press, "Text of Donald Trump's Remarks to the GOP Convention." July 22, 2016.

Conclusion

136 Michael Barone, "Donald Trump and the Outstate Midwest Redraw the Partisan Lines," syndicated column appearing December 2, 2016.

137 Ibid.

138 CNN, "Exit Polls: Florida Senate" and "Florida President", November 9, 2016.

139 Harry Enten, "Something Funny Happened in Iowa, and It May Hurt Democrats in 2016," FiveThirtyEight, November 11, 2014.

140 Sean Trende, "The Case of the Missing White Voters, Revisited," Real Clear Politics, June 21, 2013.

141 Michael Barone, "Donald Trump and the Outstate Midwest Redraw The Partisan Lines."

142 Winning 2014 and setting the Stage for 2016 Americas Majority Report December 2014, Thomas Donelson and J.D Johannes

143 Joel Kotkin A California Democrat, looks at the GOP by Tom Donelson December 15, 2015 Texas GOP Vote.com

144 Ibid.

55353982R00102

Made in the USA
Middletown, DE
09 December 2017